**Brassey's
Battlefield Weapons Systems
& Technology, Volume XI**

Military
Helicopters

Brassey's
Battlefield Weapons Systems and Technology Series

General Editor: Colonel R G Lee OBE, Former Military Director of Studies at the Royal Military College of Science, Shrivenham, UK

This new series of course manuals is written by senior lecturing staff at RMCS, Shrivenham, one of the world's foremost institutions for military science and its application. It provides a clear and concise survey of the complex systems spectrum of modern ground warfare for officers-in-training and volunteer reserves throughout the English-speaking world.

Introduction to Battlefield Weapons Systems and Technology—R G Lee

For full details of these titles in the series, please contact your local Brassey's/Pergamon office

Other Titles of Interest from Brassey's Defence Publishers

Military
Helicopters

P. G. Harrison, E. J. Everett-Heath, G. M. Moss and A. W. Mowat

Royal Military College of Science, Shrivenham, UK

BRASSEY'S DEFENCE PUBLISHERS
a member of the Pergamon Group

LONDON · OXFORD · WASHINGTON D.C. · NEW YORK
TORONTO · SYDNEY · PARIS · FRANKFURT

U.K. (Editorial)	Brassey's Defence Publishers Ltd., a member of the Pergamon Group, Maxwell House, 74 Worship Street, London EC2A 2EN
(Orders & Enquiries)	Brassey's Defence Publishers Ltd., Headington Hill Hall, Oxford OX3 0BW, England
U.S.A. (Editorial)	Pergamon-Brassey's International Defense Publishers, 1340 Old Chain Bridge Road, McLean, Virginia 22101, U.S.A.
(Orders & Enquiries)	Pergamon Press Inc., Maxwell House, Fairview Park, Elmsford, New York 10523, U.S.A.
CANADA	Pergamon Press Canada Ltd., Suite 104, 150 Consumers Road, Willowdale, Ontario M2J 1P9, Canada
AUSTRALIA	Pergamon Press (Aust.) Pty. Ltd., P.O. Box 544, Potts Point, N.S.W. 2011, Australia
FRANCE	Pergamon Press SARL, 24 rue des Ecoles, 75240 Paris, Cedex 05, France
FEDERAL REPUBLIC OF GERMANY	Pergamon Press GmbH, Hammerweg 6, D-6242 Kronberg-Taunus, Federal Republic of Germany

First edition 1985

Library of Congress Cataloging in Publication Data
Main entry under title:
Military helicopters.
(Brassey's Battlefield weapons systems and technology series; v. 11)
Bibliography: p. 151
Includes index.
1. Military helicopters. I. Harrison, P. G.
II. Series: Battlefield weapons systems & technology; v. 11.
UG1230.M55   1985   623.74'6047   84-19100

British Library Cataloguing in Publication Data
Military helicopters.—(Brassey's battlefield weapons systems and technology)
1. Military helicopters
I. Harrison, P. G.
623.74'6047   UG1230
ISBN 0-08-029958-X Hard cover
ISBN 0-08-029959-8 Flexicover

The views expressed in the book are those of the authors and not necessarily those of the Ministry of Defence of the United Kingdom.

Printed by A. Wheaton & Co. Ltd., Exeter

Preface

The Series

This series of books is written for those who wish to improve their knowledge of military weapons and equipment. It is equally relevant to professional soldiers, those involved in developing or producing military weapons or indeed anyone interested in the art of modern warfare.

All the texts are written in a way which assumes no mathematical knowledge and no more technical depth than would be gleaned from school days. It is intended that the books should be of particular interest to army officers who are studying for promotional examinations, furthering their knowledge at specialist arms schools or attending command and staff schools.

The authors of the books are members of the staff of the Royal Military College of Science, Shrivenham, which is comprised of a unique blend of academic and military experts. They are not only leaders in the technology of their subjects, but are aware of what the military practitioner needs to know. It is difficult to imagine any group of persons more fitted to write about the application of technology to the battlefield.

This Volume

A concise introduction to the principles of rotary wing flight and the characteristics and limitations of military helicopters. Technological advances are probably being made faster in aviation than any other field, and the helicopter is enjoying its share of these rapid developments. Indeed, the once fragile helicopter has been transformed into a hardened fighting machine, capable of giving and taking considerable punishment while continuing to fight. Properly exploited, air power can be a decisive, battle winning factor: helicopters have extended the overall spectrum of aviation activities and the professional soldier needs to understand their capabilities if he is to gain the maximum benefit from them. The book will also be of interest to those who seek to expand their knowledge of military helicopters beyond the normal catalogues and recognition manuals.

GEOFFREY LEE

Acknowledgements

The authors greatly appreciate the help they have received from members of many service establishments. In particular from the Royal Aircraft Establishment, Farnborough, the Army Air Corps Centre and the Mechanics and Applied Thermodynamics Branches of the Royal Military College of Science. The authors are also most grateful to Mr W. Packer, Mr C. Smith and Mr R. Bending for their assistance with diagrams.

P.G.H.
E.J.E.H.
G.M.M.
A.W.M.

Contents

List of Illustrations

Chapter 7

Chapter 8

Chapter 9

1.

History

The Early Days

Having successfully flown in a fixed wing aircraft, in December 1903, man's attention turned increasingly to the more challenging and complex problems of rotary wing flight. Visionaries had long since prophesied the possibility of machines which rose vertically into the air before changing into forward flight. The prospect excited the imagination of Leonardo da Vinci who, in 1490, designed a machine of wood and starched linen, powered by a spring mechanism, which he called a helical screw. The idea, popular with many early designers, was that the machine would literally screw itself vertically into the air. It was not clear how the return journey was to be effected! Leonardo's spiral is shown in Fig. 1.1 and it is from this machine that the word helicopter is thought, in part, to be derived: it is a combination of the Greek for spiral (helix) and wing (pteron).

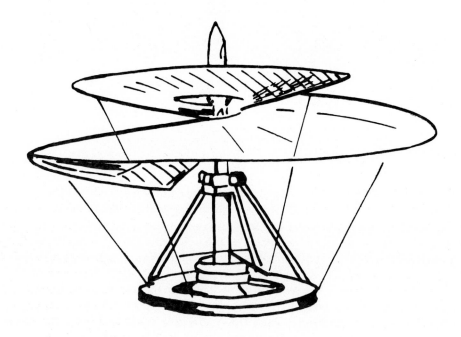

FIG. 1.1 Leonardo's spiral

Leonardo would, no doubt, have heard about, if not seen, the clever toys which could achieve vertical flight, but he could not have known that it was to be another 417 years before a piloted machine was to lift itself vertically off the ground. In the intervening years there was no shortage of inventive ideas, but the lack of a sufficiently lightweight engine producing an adequate power-to-weight ratio was the main stumbling block. The invention of the four-stroke internal combustion engine by N. A. Otto in 1876 was the major breakthrough for which aircraft designers had been waiting. By applying the principle of the Otto cycle in a 45 h.p. Antoinette engine, the Breguet-Richet Gyroplane No. 1 achieved the first successful vertical flight in September 1907. The machine, which is shown in Fig. 1.2, was built of a central chassis and four arms of tubular steel. The chassis supported the pilot and the power plant, while each arm was mounted by an eight-bladed rotor 8 m in diameter. One pair of diametrically opposed rotors rotated clockwise, the other pair anti-clockwise. The machine rose to a height of 1.5 m, but since it had to be steadied by a man at each corner, having no control nor steering devices of its own, it could not take the credit for being the first helicopter to make a truly free flight.

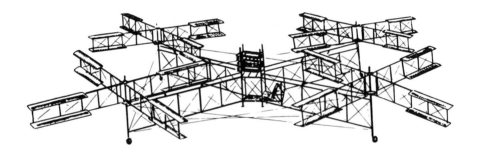

FIG. 1.2 Breguet-Richet Gyroplane No. 1

The first time vertical free flight actually took place was in November 1907 at Coquainvilliers, when Paul Cornu flew his 'flying bicycle' to an altitude of 0.3 m for 20 seconds. His machine can be seen in Fig. 1.3 and consisted of a 'V' frame on a four-wheeled undercarriage, with the pilot and the 24 h.p. Antoinette piston engine supported at the centre. At the extremities of the 'V' were two bicycle-type wheels onto which were fastened two fabric covered paddles: they were the rotor blades, 6 m in diameter. The wheels were driven by belts from a central shaft and control (such as it was) was provided by two static vanes mounted at the extreme ends of the supporting frame. This flimsy machine had a dubious transmission system and almost non-existent control. It proved so impractical that it was abandoned shortly after making its historic flight.

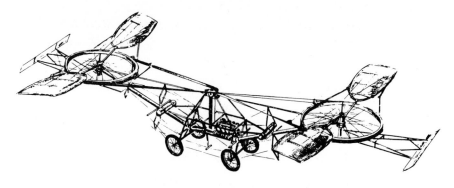

Fɪɢ. 1.3 Paul Cornu helicopter

The problem of a suitable engine had been overcome, but helicopter designers were now faced with the problem of stability and control highlighted by Paul Cornu's machine. It had been recognised for some time that a rotor having rotary momentum in one direction set up a reaction in the opposite direction in accordance with Newton's Third Law: To every action there is an equal and opposite reaction. Various methods were devised to overcome this torque reaction. The most popular was the use of coaxial rotors moving in opposite directions, around the same shaft or on individual shafts, in which the two torque reactions cancelled each other out. In 1874 Achenbach of Germany produced a design which included a tail rotor for anti-torque control; this was the first time that this now familiar device had been proposed. It was also discovered that if power for the main rotor blades was provided at the tips of the blades, rather than driving them through a control shaft, then no torque was experienced. Consequently a number of designs, ranging from steam jets or compressed air to small driving propellers, used devices placed at the ends of the main blades. Although these ideas removed the need for any anti-torque device, the method of getting energy continuously to the rotor tips was complex and difficult and was, therefore, not a popular idea.

Directional control and transition into forward flight posed special problems. Early solutions were to tilt the main rotors in a fixed position to give both vertical lift and horizontal movement (Breguet-Richet No. 2) or for the pilot to tilt the main shafts by means of cables (Denny). In 1912 Ellehammer of Denmark, one of the most brilliant of the early designers, produced a compound helicopter, seen in Fig. 1.4, which possessed many interesting and novel features. In addition to a hydraulic clutch and gearbox and its 36 h.p. radial piston engine, lift was provided by contra-rotating rotors with movable vanes at the extremity of each. By changing the angle of the vanes, the pilot could alter the direction of flight, and this was one of the earliest and most successful examples of a pilot exercising positive control in flight.

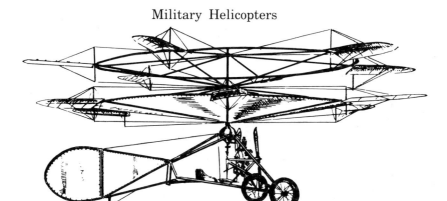

Fig. 1.4 Ellehammer 1912

This aircraft crashed in 1916 and Ellehammer put aside his helicopter experiments until 1930.

The early 1920s saw several interesting projects of which the most promising was Pescara's No. 3 machine: it can be seen in Fig. 1.5. This ponderous looking machine represented a major step forward in helicopter technology because the eight pairs of blades in its contra-rotating rotor system could be controlled in flight to produce increased lift, and the rotor head could be tilted to produce forward flight. Although only modest speeds were achieved, this aircraft was the first to provide a convincing demonstration of controlling both lift and direction of flight. Pescara also showed that he was one of the first to understand autorotation, since his aircraft was designed to descend safely should the engine fail. The aircraft established a world distance record of 736 m and was considered to be a relatively simple machine when compared with its very complex contemporaries.

Fig. 1.5 Pescara No. 3

Juan de la Cierva

In 1919 the Spaniard who, it is said, laid the foundations on which the modern helicopter stands hit upon a remarkable idea. Near accidents involving both himself and his brother in their early flying careers had been caused mainly by stall: so he made a great study of this problem. He reasoned that a rotating aerofoil produces lift in much the same way as a fixed aerofoil which moves forward through the air and, therefore, it should be possible to replace one by the other. The great difference between his idea and all that had gone before is that his windmills or rotors were to be freely rotating and not driven by the engine. Engine power would be used to drive a conventional propeller to provide forward thrust and to run the rotating blades up to a speed where they would produce sufficient lift for take-off. Thereafter, the airflow produced by the aircraft's forward speed would cause the rotor to turn freely and thus generate lift without any contribution from the engine. He called his invention the Autogyro. His first design is shown in Fig. 1.6.

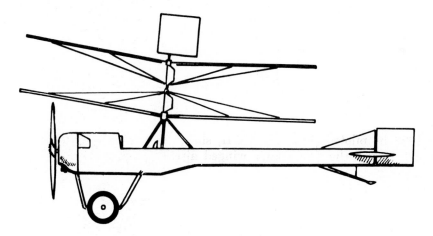

FIG. 1.6 Cierva's Autogyro

A freely rotating rotor which produces lift from a flow of air is said to be in a state of autorotation, and it will be readily appreciated that since there is no drive through the rotor shaft to set up a torque reaction, that one of the main problems which bedevilled early helicopters designers simply did not exist in Autogyros. However, Cierva found that his designs still suffered from a second major problem called disymmetry of lift. It had been discovered that if a machine with a rotor was moving forward through the air, this affected the blades of the rotor in two ways. First, the blade which was rotating from the tail to the nose, i.e. which was advancing, experienced not only its own rotational speed but also the speed of the aircraft through the air. Second, it is obvious from the preceding statement that the blade rotating from nose to tail, i.e. the retreating blade, experienced an opposite effect, its rotational speed minus the forward speed of the aircraft. Thus since lift is partly a function of speed, the advancing blade produces more lift than the retreating blade and the aircraft tends to roll towards the retreating blade where less lift is being produced. After many fruitless attempts to overcome this seemingly intractable problem, Cierva invented a vertical hinge for each rotor blade, which allowed the advancing blade to flap up, giving less lift, and the retreating blade to flap down, giving more lift. Thus the unequal lift between the blades was eliminated and this, the flapping hinge, shown in Fig. 1.7 was, arguably, his greatest contribution to aviation.

After a number of years spent modifying and improving his designs, another serious problem was overcome by Cierva. He found that his flapping hinges caused severe oscillations at the roots of the blades and he designed a further hinge which allowed each blade a certain amount of movement in azimuth. These he called drag hinges, and they can be seen on many helicopters to this day; they are described in detail in Chapter 2.

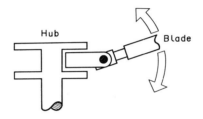

FIG. 1.7 Flapping hinge

In 1928 he piloted the C.8L Mk II, shown in Fig. 1.8, across the English Channel. It was the first rotary winged aircraft to do this.

FIG. 1.8 Cierva C.8L Mk II

It will be seen in Fig. 1.8 that the C.8L has conventional in addition to rotary wings. Autogyros are characterised by a conventional propeller, fuselage and tail section, but may or may not have fixed wings; many early designs had coaxial rotors. Modern versions are small, highly manoeuvrable, reliable and cheap to operate. Their major drawback, as potential military machines, is their inability to maintain a hover. Even so, Cierva's contribution to aviation and to helicopters in particular was of great importance.

1930 Onwards

Despite the development of gyroplanes and improvements of early helicopters, it was not until 1936 that the first convincing demonstration was made of a practical helicopter. This was the German Focke-Wulf FW61, which went on to demonstrate an autorotative landing and also to achieve several world records a year later. The world was astonished by its first indoor demonstration in Berlin in the same year. A photograph of this demonstration is shown in Fig. 1.9.

Fig. 1.9 FW61's indoor demonstration—Berlin 1937

The next major development was the production of the S 300 in America by Igor Sikorsky. It was the first to use the main and tail rotor configuration successfully and was the forerunner of the R4 shown in Fig. 1.10, which marked the beginning of helicopter manufacture in the USA. This unique aircraft, which first flew in 1942, had side-by-side seating for two pilots and was to demonstrate, for the first time, the real potential of the helicopter to the world.

FIG. 1.10 Sikorsky R4

Although it was now widely recognised that the helicopter had arrived and had a valuable part to play in general aviation, the true worth of military helicopters only became apparent in the 1950s. They were used extensively by the French Army in Algeria, by the American Army in Korea and by the British Army in the Far East. Although the tasks performed by these aircraft were mainly observation and reconnaissance, casualty evacuation and movement of men and materiel, their use as weapons platforms was also being investigated. The attraction of being able to move weapons rapidly about the battlefield was attractive to military leaders, although some placed too much emphasis on the vulnerability of the aircraft, disregarding its ability to fly very low, nap-of-the-earth, and to hover behind cover out of sight of an enemy.

The war in Vietnam provided the United States with a situation and terrain which were well suited to helicopter operations. Medium and heavy lift helicopters and the ubiquitous utility helicopter all played important parts in this war, although it was, perhaps, the coming of age of the helicopter gunship which was of most interest. For those who maintained that the helicopter was too vulnerable to survive on a modern battlefield, the statistics proved interesting. Very few helicopters were lost as a result of enemy anti-aircraft fire, and this against a proliferation of small arms and heavy MGs and also against sophisticated AA missiles. The US Army had no doubt that the helicopter had proved its worth as a battlefield weapon.

Since then, helicopters have been used in active service operations by the Soviet Union, confirming, in particular, their value as flexible effective weapons platforms. They have been used continuously by the British Army and RAF in

Northern Ireland and they were used extensively by the Royal Navy and the Army recently in the Falklands. Indeed it is true to say that they played a very important part in bringing this latter conflict to a successful conclusion and commanders wanted more.

The two major helicopter-producing countries, the USA and the Soviet Union, have no doubts that helicopters will play a leading part in any future war. Accordingly, they have equipped their armies, navies and airforces with large numbers of various types of special to role helicopters. Other West European countries, while no less enthusiastic, are constrained by economics to fewer numbers and types. It follows that most of their helicopters will be expected to perform a number of roles.

2.
Principles of Flight

Introduction

For a helicopter to fly, its total weight must be overcome by a lifting force. This force is produced by air flowing over the main rotor blades and is similar to the way that lift is generated by a fixed wing, but by rotary rather than linear movement.

Definitions

To assist in understanding rotary wing aerodynamics, a few simple definitions should be known. Some are illustrated in Fig. 2.1.

Chord Line

A chord line is a straight line joining the leading and trailing edges of an aerofoil.

Relative Air Flow (RAF)

The relative air flow is the motion of air relative to an aerofoil.

Angle of Attack

The angle of attack is the angle measured between the chord line and the relative air flow.

Pitch Angle

The pitch angle is the acute angle between the chord line and the rotor plane of rotation.

Centre of Pressure

The centre of pressure is the point on the chord line through which the resultant of all surface forces on a rotor blade act.

Rotor Disc

The rotor disc is a circle described by the tips of the rotor blades. This is also known as the tip path plane.

Total Rotor Thrust

Total rotor thrust is the sum of the lift produced by the rotor blades. It acts at right angles to the rotor disc.

Coning

Coning is the angle between the rotor blades and the horizontal, caused by increasing the load on the blades. It is most noticeable when a large helicopter is taking off.

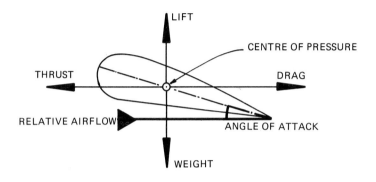

FIG. 2.1 Definitions

The Atmosphere

It is worth mentioning, briefly, the importance of the atmosphere to flying machines. This is an ocean of air which surrounds the earth; it is a compressible fluid and as such is able to flow or change its shape when subjected even to the smallest pressures. One of its most important properties is that density decreases with height, which has an adverse effect on the lift generated by an aerofoil and also on engine performance at altitude.

The important parameters for aerodynamic flight depend on the mass density of the air, the static pressure and the static temperature. In a fluid, static pressures and temperatures are measured by instruments which are stationary with respect to the fluid. Two other quantities which are important for flight are the speed of sound and the coefficient of viscosity. They both depend only on air temperature.

The International Standard Atmosphere (ISA) is a model atmosphere which is used for aircraft and missile performance calculations. It approximates to the average conditions in Europe and North America. The essential assumption is that the temperature at all heights is prescribed. The sea level temperature is 15°C. It then falls by 6.5°C per 1000 m increase in height for the first 11,000 m. This region is known as the Troposphere, and it is in this region that helicopters operate.

Lift

An aerofoil section, whether fixed or rotary wing, generates lift in accordance with Bernoulli's Theorem which states:

In the streamline flow of an ideal fluid energy remains constant.

Or put more simply:

Movement (Kinetic) Energy + Pressure Energy = a constant.

It follows from this that if speed increases, pressure will decrease and vice versa. Taking a simple aerofoil shape, it can be seen that speed (s) and pressure (p) vary as shown in Fig. 2.2.

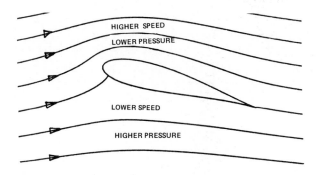

FIG. 2.2 Variations in speed and pressure over an aerofoil

As the air flow speeds up over the more rounded upper surface there is a significant drop in pressure. The effect of this will be to lift the aerofoil towards the area of lower pressure, at right angles to the air flow. If the angle of attack is changed, the pressure distribution around the aerofoil changes as shown in Fig. 2.3.

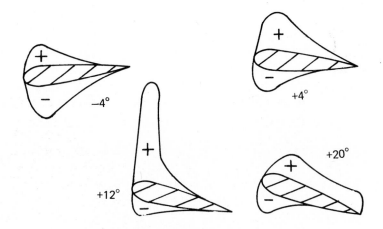

FIG. 2.3 Pressure distribution at different angles of attack

It follows, therefore, that lift increases as the angle of attack increases up to an angle of approximately 15°. Thereafter, drag increases rapidly and lift falls away until the aerofoil stalls. This effect is shown in the graph at Fig. 2.4.

Increased lift can also be achieved by setting an aerofoil at a constant pitch angle then speeding up its movement through the air. Helicopter rotors, however, contain considerable inertia, which make rotor speed adjustments a slow and unacceptable method of altering lift.

Since helicopters have a number of rotor blades, it is necessary to increase the angle of attack of all of them uniformly if equal lift is to be generated by each blade. This is achieved by the pilot, who raises a lever which will increase the angle of attack of all the blades at the same time: it is known as applying pitch. The lever is called the collective pitch lever and is linked mechanically through control rods in the fuselage to the rotor head. There, the controls are linked to a device called swash plates, one fixed and one which revolves with the rotor blades, which increase or decrease pitch. Movement up or down of the non-rotating plate causes the rotating plate also to move up or down, regardless of tilt, changing the pitch angle of all the blades collectively, as shown in Fig. 2.5.

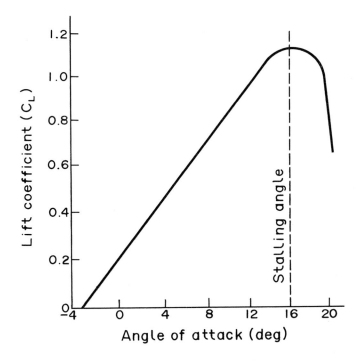

FIG. 2.4 Variation of lift with angle of attack

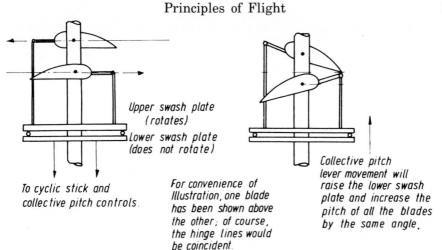

Upper swash plate
(rotates)

Lower swash plate
(does not rotate)

To cyclic stick and
collective pitch controls.

For convenience of
Illustration, one blade
has been shown above
the other; of course,
the hinge lines would
be coincident.

Collective pitch
lever movement will
raise the lower swash
plate and increase the
pitch of all the blades
by the same angle.

FIG. 2.5 How the swash plate changes pitch

Alternative methods can be used to change pitch although the swash plate principle is most commonly used: the principles are similar. The collective lever is normally positioned to be operated by the left hand and it works in the normal sense—as the lever is raised, the helicopter rises and vice versa.

Drag

Any body, such as an aerofoil, which moves through the air experiences a force which acts to resist such movement. This is called drag and it acts parallel to the air flow. The resistance encountered depends partly on the extent to which the object disrupts the smooth flow of air; as would be expected, it is higher for a flat plate at right angles to the air flow than for a sphere.

By changing the shape of a body in an air flow, known as streamlining, drag can be reduced markedly. This is shown in Fig. 2.6.

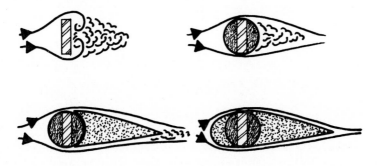

Fig. 2.6 The effect of streamlining

The origins of drag are complex, but it appears in two basic forms, induced drag and profile drag. Induced drag can be simply described as that drag created by lift —it is the penalty for having lift. Profile drag occurs partly because of the shape of the body in the air flow, i.e. form drag, and also consists of skin friction. When there is relative motion between a body and the air, skin friction causes a thin layer of air closest to the body to become retarded. This is known as the boundary layer and it plays an important part in determining the characteristics of the aerofoil, particularly the stalling characteristics and the maximum lift which can be produced.

Having produced a simple graph to illustrate lift, it is also possible to produce a similar graph to illustrate total drag. This is shown in Fig. 2.7 and it shows how drag increases slowly with angle of attack up to the angle of stall, after which it increases sharply.

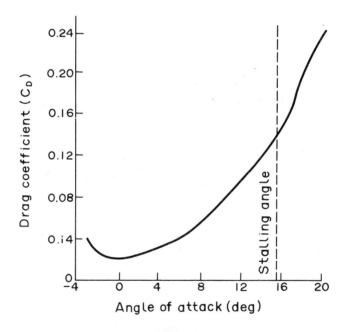

FIG. 2.7 Variation of drag with angle of attack

By combining the readings of the two graphs showing variations of lift and drag with angle of attack, it will be seen that the most efficient angle of attack is about 4°, as shown in Fig. 2.8. It will also be seen that the aerofoil becomes less efficient after this point and its performance falls away quite dramatically from about 11° to the angle of stall. This characteristic is common to both rotating and fixed aerofoils.

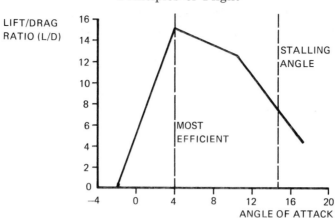

Fig. 2.8 Variation of lift/drag with angle of attack

The Four Forces

There are four forces which act on a fixed wing aircraft in flight: lift, drag, weight and thrust. When considering a helicopter, however, these are reduced to three: rotor thrust, weight and parasite drag. Parasite drag is the sum of the drag forces on all the components of the helicopter, excluding the rotor, and since it increases as the square of the forward speed, considerable rotor thrust must be generated as forward speeds increase.

Thrust

If the rotor disc of a conventional helicopter is tilted in any direction, the total rotor thrust will also be angled in the same direction and the aircraft will tend to move along that line. The tilt is achieved by causing one blade to rise and the opposite blade to fall, which effectively tips the rotor disc and total rotor thrust in the same direction. In Fig. 2.9 the rear blade has risen and the front blade has lowered: consequently the rotor disc tilts towards the front of the helicopter, which then moves forward.

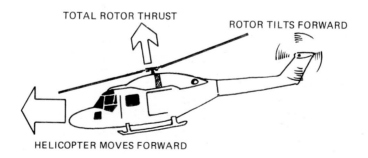

Fig. 2.9 Transition forward

MH–C

To keep the disc tilted, the pitch angle of the blades must vary from a low to a
high setting throughout the 360° cycle of travel. This is known as cyclic pitch
change: it occurs when the pilot moves the cyclic pitch stick with his right hand,
again in a natural sense. As he pushes the stick forward, the helicopter moves
forward, and as he moves it backwards the helicopter moves back. The controls
run from the stick parallel to those from the collective lever, along the fuselage
and up to the rotor head. Here there are several ways of changing the pitch of the
blades to achieve directional flight, the most common is to tilt the swash plate as
shown in Fig. 2.10. It will be recalled that the swash plate is also used to make
collective pitch changes.

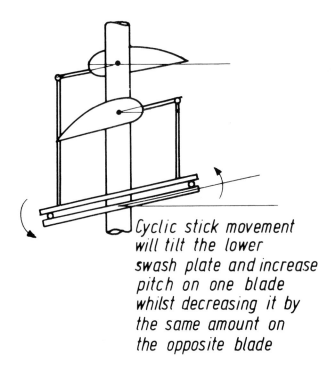

Cyclic stick movement
will tilt the lower
swash plate and increase
pitch on one blade
whilst decreasing it by
the same amount on
the opposite blade

FIG. 2.10 The swash plate method of transmitting cyclic pitch changes

Hinges

During the early development of the helicopter it was found necessary to
incorporate three types of hinge into the main rotor. It will be recalled from
Chapter 1 that to overcome the problems of disymmetry of lift in forward flight, a
flapping hinge was invented by Cierva, and he followed this by introducing a
drag hinge to overcome the problems of oscillations in his autogyros. A feathering
hinge was also introduced later to allow pitch changes to be made by the pilot.
Figure 2.11 shows how those three types of hinge work. A rotor head with all
these features is called a fully articulated rotor.

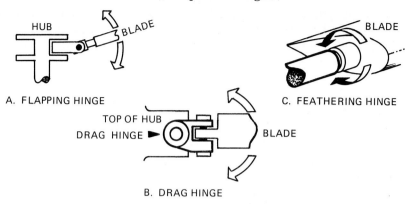

HUB

BLADE

A. FLAPPING HINGE

BLADE

C. FEATHERING HINGE

TOP OF HUB

DRAG HINGE ▶

BLADE

B. DRAG HINGE

FIG. 2.11 Flapping, drag and feathering hinges

More modern helicopters enjoy the advantages of new materials which have simplified rotor head design. The rotor head of the Westland Lynx, for example, is machined from a solid titanium block and has titanium arms attached inboard of the blades. It is said to be a hingeless or semi-rigid rotor head and the flexibility of the titanium arms does away with the need for either a flapping or drag hinge. Feathering is achieved by twisting the only hinge in the system which attaches the rotor blade to the dog bone, so called because of its obvious shape, shown in Fig. 2.12.

FIG. 2.12 Lynx semi-rigid rotor head

It is also possible to go one step further by constructing a rotor head without any hinges whatever, in which all control movements are transmitted through bending parts of the rotor head. Such a configuration is called a bearingless or rigid rotor.

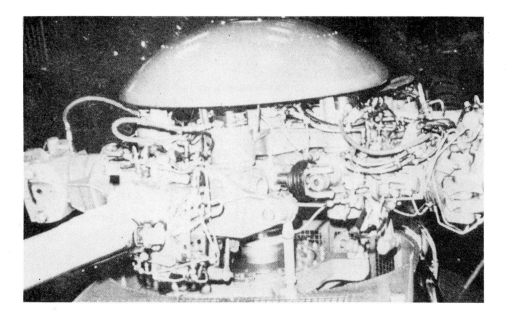

Fig. 2.13 Sea King main rotor head

By their very nature, rotor heads are complex pieces of engineering, and this is very well illustrated by the Westland Sea King's rotor head shown in Fig. 2.13. This has the additional complexity of a hydraulic blade folding system added to it.

Countering Torque

Counter Rotation

So far we can see that the helicopter can lift off the ground and move in any direction, but it will be remembered from Chapter 1 that the rotor blades moving around the main shaft set up an equal and opposite reaction on the fuselage, called torque. If nothing were done to counter this, the fuselage would rotate in the opposite direction to the blades and normal flight would be impossible. There are several ways of eliminating torque, one of which is to mount counter-rotating rotor blades on control shafts. In this system one set of rotor blades intermeshes with the other and their torque effects cancel out each other. This method is used in the American Kaman HH43B helicopter shown in Fig. 2.14.

Fɪɢ. 2.14 Kaman HH43B

Twin Rotors

Another method of achieving the same effect is used by the American CH-47 Chinook helicopter, which has twin rotors, each mounted on its own shaft, and each rotating in the opposite direction. This technique is shown in Fig. 2.15.

Fig. 2.15 CH-47 Chinook

Advancing Blade

The most advanced twin-rotor design can be seen on the Sikorsky XH-59A advancing blade concept (ABC). This consists of two rigid, coaxial, counter-rotating rotors, which, because of their special design characteristics, enable the aircraft to fly at much higher forward speeds than other helicopters. This aircraft is still in the design phase at present, and is shown in Fig. 2.16. It is referred to in more detail in Chapter 9.

Fig. 2.16 The Sikorsky XH-59A ABC

Directional control in twin-rotor helicopters is achieved by applying more torque
to one rotor shaft than the other, creating a torque differential which will rotate
the fuselage; or by tilting the rotors in opposition to each other.

Tail Rotor

The conventional anti-torque device is the tail rotor. This may be a pusher or
puller, depending on which side of the tail fin it is mounted. It is driven from the
main gearbox through drive shafts and its own smaller gearboxes, and will
therefore, normally rotate when the main rotor is rotating. The pilot can alter the
collective pitch of the tail rotor by using his rudder pedals and thus increasing or
decreasing the tail rotor blades angles of attack. In this way their overall effect
can turn the fuselage left or right about the axis of the main rotor. A typical tail
rotor assembly is shown in Fig. 2.17.

FIG. 2.17 A typical tail rotor

Tail rotors incur a drag penalty in forward flight which led to Aerospatiale
designing a tail rotor which was completely enclosed within the tail fin. Although
this could be more accurately described as a ducted fan, it has exactly the same
effect as a conventional tail rotor and is operated in the same way. A Gazelle tail
rotor, called a fenestron, is shown in Fig. 2.18. It is less efficient than a
conventional tail rotor in the hover, but is more efficient in forward flight.

FIG. 2.18 Gazelle fenestron

Effect of Controls

By putting together the effects of the collective pitch, cyclic stick and tail rotor controls, it is possible to see exactly how flight is achieved and what actions are needed by the pilot to maintain control. This is shown diagrammatically in Fig. 2.19.

It will be seen that for almost every manoeuvre executed by the helicopter that the pilot needs to make continual corrections with all three controls. It is for this reason that automatic systems, designed to reduce the pilot's work load, have been introduced. These systems work in pitch, roll and yaw and are called automatic flight control systems (AFCS) or, in a more simple form, stabilised augmentation systems (SAS). They are covered in more detail in Chapter 5.

Autorotation

Should the only engine of a single engined helicopter fail in flight, the main rotor takes on the function of the blades of an autogyro by continuing to rotate and providing lift without any contribution from the engine. The difference between this and the normal flight condition is that the flow of air through the main rotor is upwards instead of downwards. This upward flow keeps the rotors running at high speed and allows the pilot to glide to earth. At about 200 feet

FLIGHT REGIME	ACTIONS BY PILOT	EFFECTS
From ground to hover	 Keeps Stick Central — Raises Lever. Balance torque with rudder pedals	Blades cone up with increased pitch. 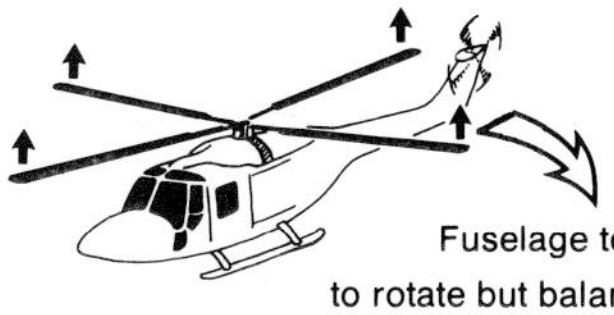 Fuselage tends to rotate but balanced by increase in tail rotor pitch
Transition from hover to forward flight	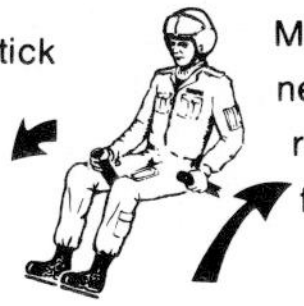 Pushes stick forward. More lift needed so raises lever further. More pedal to balance increase in torque	Blades cone up further. 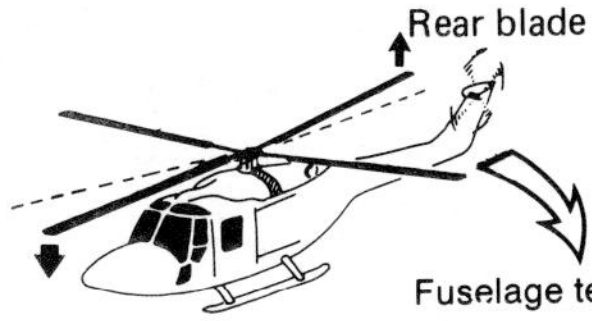 Rear blade flaps up. Forward blade flaps down. Fuselage tends to rotate further but balanced by tail rotor
Cruise flight	 Trims stick to balance datum. Locks lever to required pitch setting. Maintains balanced flight with rudder pedals	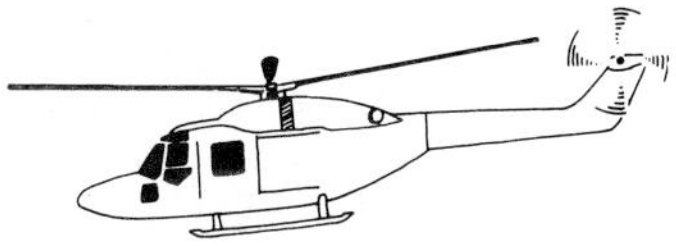 Aircraft enters balanced forward flight condition
Descending flight	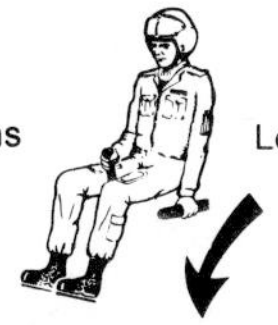 Maintains forward flight. Lowers lever. Applies opposite rudder pedal to reduce anti-torque	Blades cone down. 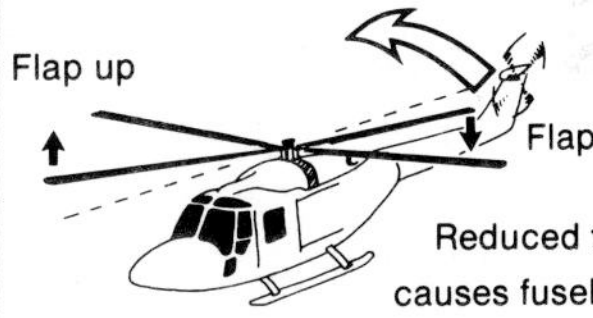 Flap up. Flap down. Reduced torque causes fuselage to move in opposite direction
Spot turn in hover	 Maintains hover over central spot with stick. Slight adjustments to maintain height with lever. Depresses rudder pedal in direction of turn	 Fuselage moves round axis of main hub

FIG. 2.19 How a helicopter is controlled

above the ground the pilot will reduce his forward speed by moving the cyclic stick to the rear; this is known as flaring. Then by levelling the fuselage and using the energy remaining in the rotor, he uses the collective lever to cushion the aircraft on to the ground, normally touching down at a low forward speed. A zero forward speed autorotative landing is also possible. Thus a safe landing without power can easily be made, albeit with an initial high rate of descent. It is unlikely that a twin-engined helicopter would suffer a double engine failure and be faced with an autorotative landing, but should both engines fail, the same technique already described would be used.

Types and Configurations

In addition to the conventional helicopter and autogyro already mentioned, compound helicopters have also been designed and flown. These are helicopters which derive a substantial part of their lift and thrust from a powered rotor but which have, in addition, fixed wings, additional propulsive systems, or both. A sketch of a typical compound design is shown in Fig. 2.20.

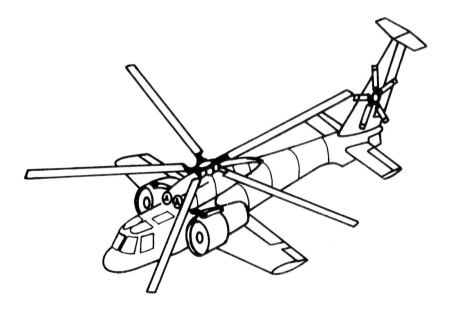

FIG. 2.20 A typical compound helicopter

Many different configurations have been tried; six are shown in Fig. 2.21. Design has tended to stabilise on the conventional main and tail rotor layout, although there are other types still in service.

Helicopter aerodynamics is a complex, subject which has been covered in outline only in this chapter. However, the basic fundamentals are common to all types of helicopter and must be understood if the capabilities and limitations of these machines are to be appreciated.

(a) Single-rotor helicopter
    with tail rotor

(b) Tandem

(c) Tandem overlapping

(d) Side-by-side
    non-intermeshing

(e) Co-axial contra-rotating

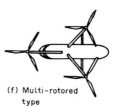

(f) Multi-rotored
    type

FIG. 2.21 Configurations

SELF TEST QUESTIONS

QUESTION 1   What are the main effects of increased altitude on helicopter performance?

Answer ....

....

....

QUESTION 2   How does an aerofoil shape generate lift?

Answer ....

....

....

QUESTION 3   What is the maximum angle of attack at which lift is generated?

Answer ....

QUESTION 4   What happens after this maximum angle is exceeded?

Answer ....

....

....

QUESTION 5   How does a helicopter rise vertically into a hover?

Answer ....

....

....

....

....

QUESTION 6   In what forms does drag appear?

Answer ....

....

....

QUESTION 7   How does a helicopter move forwards and backwards when in a hover?

Answer ....

....

....

QUESTION 8   How many hinges are there in a fully articulated rotor head and what are they?

Answer ....

....

....

QUESTION 9   How is torque countered in a conventional helicopter?

Answer ....

....

....

QUESTION 10 What is meant by autorotation?

Answer ....

....

....

Answers on page 133

3.

Roles

Roles

The versatility of the helicopter became apparent during the Korean War and they were soon being used for a variety of tasks, both civilian and military. The military roles do not differ markedly between nations, it is only the priority accorded to each role which tends to be different.

Observation and Reconnaissance

The Need

Observation and reconnaissance is traditionally a most important role carried out by army helicopters and their crews, and it is still rated as the most important in many armies. It stems from the need of commanders to acquire short-term information about the enemy, and to be able to see their future positions and likely engagement areas quickly. Both aspects demand good optical aids, particularly in the observation role, if the helicopter is to stay as far away from the enemy as possible, out of range of his ground-based anti-air weapons.

Binocular Systems

The first step in extending the pilot's natural eyesight was to use standard binoculars: this was best done by an observer, since the pilot was fully occupied with flying the aircraft. These devices were found to be useful, but far from satisfactory because helicopters always tend to vibrate a great deal, and the inevitable movement of the airframe in flight meant that the image seen through the binoculars could not be held steady and was almost continuously blurred. It was found that by fitting soft rubber eyepieces and, more important, by stabilising the binoculars, the image became much more distinct. The stabilising gyroscope was driven from the aircraft's electrical system and the whole device was small enough to be suspended below the binoculars without hindrance, as shown in Fig. 3.1. They are still in use today.

FIG. 3.1 Kenlab stabilised binoculars

Stabilising the whole device was cumbersome, however effective, and there soon appeared another device which stabilised only a mirror inside the case, through which the image of the target was fed to the observer. This was produced by BAC and called the Steadyscope, shown in Fig. 3.2. It is much lighter than the stabilised binoculars while achieving a similar effect.

FIG. 3.2 The BAC Steadyscope

Roof Mounted Sights

At about the same time, various sights had been produced for anti-tank helicopters, for both target acquisition and missile guidance. The benefits of such sights and particularly of the Avimo-Ferranti roof-mounted AF120 sight for the British Army Air Corps, shown in Fig. 3.3, soon became apparent.

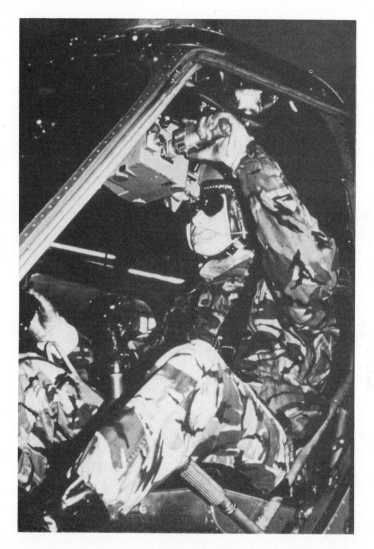

FIG. 3.3 The Avimo-Ferranti AF120 sight in a British Army Scout

Not only was the sight fully stabilised and gave $\times 2\frac{1}{2}$ and $\times 10$ magnification, but its position in the roof meant that the aircraft could observe from behind cover while exposing only the sight head and the rotors. Although it has taken some time to apply this principle to observation helicopters, there are now

MH–D

several solutions available, of which the AF532 for the Gazelle helicopter in Fig. 3.4 is one, which is expected to enter service soon.

FIG. 3.4 The AF532 sight

This sight has a stabilised mirror in its optical unit and gives ×2½ and ×10 magnification. It also has space provision for a laser target marker and range finder, a forward looking infrared (FLIR) camera for night vision, and a camera for training which can also be used as a daylight TV tracker.

Mast Mounted Sights

Although roof mounted sights represented a major step forward for the observation helicopter, it is not the end of the story. A helicopter which exposes its rotors above cover can still be detected by radar and it is logical to try to keep the whole aircraft hidden, analogous to the turret down position of a tank. To this end, mast mounted sights are under development in the USA and a typical example is the Martin-Marietta sight shown in Fig. 3.5.

FIG. 3.5 Martin-Marietta mast mounted sight

This sight weighs about 70 lb and there is another 125 lb of electronic equipment inside the helicopter. It has an optical sight with × 1¼ and ×10 magnification plus a laser range finder/designator and an automatic vidicon TV tracker. The sight head measures 16in × 14in ×7in, extends 2 feet above the rotor head, and the sensors feed a CRT display in front of the observer. Clearly such a sight will not only greatly increase the observer's capability to locate and watch the enemy but will also be a considerable aid to the survival of the helicopter.

Other Devices

TV cameras, sometimes called heli-tele, can be mounted either inside the cabin or externally for use in internal security or limited war situations. Such devices can keep a continuous watch over an area, transmitting the information to a number of ground stations. The ability of the camera to zoom in for close-ups of specific targets is of particular benefit to ground observers who can interpret the information in peaceful surroundings well away from the scene of action. This device has proved particularly successful in monitoring traffic and riot situations, and an improved camera pod for external use on Lynx is in Fig. 3.6.

FIG. 3.6 Heli-tele on a Westland Lynx

Normal hand-held cameras may also be used from helicopters, primarily for use in peacetime or in situations where the anti-air threat is low. Whatever observation or surveillance devices are used from helicopters, they should more than match the capabilities of devices used on the ground, if they are to stand back from the Forward Edge of the Battle Area (FEBA) and be able to use the additional range gained from elevating the device.

Armed Action

Suitability for the Role
This role is viewed by many to have taken over from observation and reconnaissance as the most important role of the helicopter. The ability to move faster than any other battlefield vehicle, unencumbered by terrain, is a quality which the helicopter alone possesses. It is possible for a number of different types of weapons to be carried, either built-in to the aircraft or added later as a temporary fitting, and for those weapons to be moved quickly and used at critical points on the battlefield is an advantage which few commanders would surrender lightly.

Anti-tank Guided Weapons (ATGW)

The main weapon carried, which is ideal for helicopters because of its relatively low weight and its lack of recoil, is the anti-tank guided missile. The long range of such missiles allows the helicopter to stand-off while delivering its attack and this, plus its ability to aim and fire these weapons almost totally concealed behind cover, make it a difficult target to acquire and hit. Figure 3.7 shows a Lynx helicopter, firing a TOW missile from a typical, concealed fire position.

FIG. 3.7 Lynx firing a TOW missile from ambush

Attack Helicopters

The USA and USSR both believe that not only will the helicopter be able to survive in the forward battle area but that a suitably armoured and armed helicopter will be able to conduct operations across the FEBA as a matter of course. Such a philosophy, backed by adequate finance, has resulted in both nations producing dedicated attack helicopters. Since these are likely to be attacking a variety of targets, they are armed with rockets and cannon in addition to anti-tank missiles. They are also well armoured. The crew, engines and certain critical components are protected, with other parts, such as main rotor blades, designed to withstand hits from 23 mm cannon. These helicopters also contain advanced avionics equipment which will enable them to fly and fire their weapons effectively by day and night and in bad weather. The most recent additions to the inventory of both these countries is the Apache (AH-64) in the USA, shown in Fig. 3.8, and the Mi-24 HIND in the USSR, shown in Fig. 3.9.

FIG. 3.8 The AH-64 Apache

FIG. 3.9 Mi-24 Hind

Chapter 7 deals with helicopters as weapons platforms in greater detail.

Direction of Fire

Again, traditionally, the adjustment of gunfire onto a target, whether land based, naval or delivered by Fighter Ground Attack (FGA) aircraft, has been an important function of helicopter crews. It could be argued that this is solely a crew function, but the helicopter does provide the means of getting a Forward Observation Officer (FOO) or a Forward Air Controller (FAC) to the critical point from which he can conduct his activity, and so its importance should not be overlooked.

Movement of Men and Materiel

In the same way that weapons can be freely moved about the battlefield, so troops and stores can also be lifted from point to point quickly and easily. The scale of lift depends on the size and payload of the helicopters involved and on the numbers of aircraft available. While most British Army helicopters are small by comparison with US and USSR machines, Lynx can lift up to nine fully armed troops. Medium lift is provided by the RAF's Puma and Chinook, which can lift 16 and 33 troops respectively, although a Chinook in the Falklands campaign carried almost three times this number in a single lift.

A Chinook is shown in Fig. 3.10. It is particularly well designed as a troop or load lifter. It has a large fuselage with a bottom hinged ramp at the rear of the aircraft to facilitate easy, obstruction-free access for loading vehicles or stores. In addition to its normal loads, Chinook can carry 24 stretchers in the casualty evacuation role, which is another important function of all load carrying and utility helicopters.

FIG. 3.10 A Chinook medium lift helicopter

Other NATO countries tend to keep their medium and heavy lift helicopters under army command, with types such as Puma and Chinook, providing medium lift. The CH-53 and the CH-54 Skycrane are the USA's heavy lift giants: the Skycrane is shown in Fig. 3.11.

FIG. 3.11 CH-54 Skycrane heavy lift helicopter

Large loads which are within the capability of the helicopter to carry, but either undesirable or too bulky to be carried inside it, can be underslung beneath the fuselage on a cargo hook. This hook is stressed to carry heavy weights and is anchored to hard points in the fuselage directly beneath the rotor head, at the centre of gravity. Figure 3.12 shows a British Army Lynx carrying a large load of mines in a rack suspended from its cargo hook.

The USSR, mainly because of the need to move large groups of civilians and heavy freight across the vast internal tracts of Russia, have developed a family of enormous helicopters capable of carrying quite staggering weights. All these helicopters have military counterparts and those in service with Aeroflot can easily be converted for military use. In 1965 the Mi-10 appeared, with a take-off weight of 43,700 kg over 155 miles at a maximum speed of 124 mph; this is shown in Fig. 3.13.

FIG. 3.12 Lynx with underslung mine rack

FIG. 3.13 Mi-10

Then in 1971 the amazing Mi-12 was demonstrated at Le Bourget. This enormous aircraft has a maximum take-off weight of 105,000 kg over 310 miles at 161 mph. Each of the two rotors measures 35 m in diameter and the large, rear-loading ramp would be ideal for heavy military equipment. This aircraft is shown in Fig. 3.14. However, for technical reasons it never entered production.

Finally, the USSR have now produced the Mi-26, which is the largest military helicopter in the world, codenamed HALO, shown in Fig. 3.15. It can carry up to 99 fully equipped troops or two light tanks at speeds up to 180mph for 500 miles in its fuselage, which is larger than the loading bays of many Western fixed wing transport aircraft.

FIG. 3.14 Mi-12

FIG. 3.15 Mi-26

Clearly the Russians believe that the heavy lift helicopter has an important part to play in their overall concept of operations, and their ability to carry out substantial air mobile operations is obvious.

Command and Control

Fighting a battle from a helicopter is not to every commander's liking but it is possible to provide airborne command posts (CP) in most types of utility helicopter: that for the Lynx is shown schematically at Fig. 3.16. However, most commanders prefer to use these aircraft as airborne rovers.

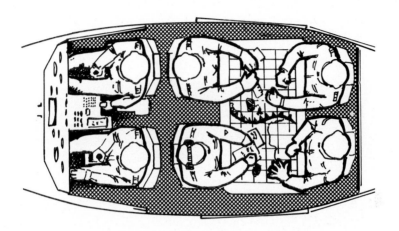

FIG. 3.16 Lynx airborne command post

For airmobile operations it is sensible for the commander to be in an airborne CP with the appropriate staff and radio sets available to him. These can include a secure speech facility when necessary. Most nations who possess an effective airmobile capability will provide this facility for the initial phase of an airmobile operation and thereafter as required.

During periods of electronic silence, helicopters can be invaluable in carrying information between HQs, moving liaison officers or larger groups to briefings, which, although not something which is widely practised in peacetime, could be an important function in a war. Helicopters can also be used as electronic warfare platforms, a practice popular in both the USA and USSR.

Naval Roles

Early Warning Platforms

Naval use of helicopters is just as widespread as their use over land, and most of the larger ships now carry at least one. The ability of the helicopter to range far out from its parent ship to provide early warning of both surface and sub-surface attack and to attack such targets is a valuable adjunct to the ship's own weapons systems. Again, this was amply demonstrated in the 1982 Falklands campaign and has led to discussion of their use as airborne early warning (AEW) systems platforms.

Anti-submarine Warfare (ASW) Platforms

In the anti-submarine warfare role, either dunking sonar, shown in Fig. 3.17, can be used, or remote sonar buoys can be dropped in the area of the target to pinpoint its location. Other devices such as a Magnetic Anomaly Detector (MAD) can also be used for the same purpose. Having located the target, it is then generally attacked by torpedo, which is dropped from the helicopter by parachute.

FIG. 3.17 A Sea King dunking its sonar

In the anti-surface vessel (ASV) role, the helicopter generally locates its target by radar, then launches its attack by guided missile. The Lynx's Seaspray radar and Sea Skua missile are typical of such weapons systems. Clearly the relatively low payload of helicopters restricts the amount of electronic equipment that can be carried and also restricts the size and, therefore, the range of its missiles. Even so, the short-range, sea skimming capability of Sea Skua fitted to Lynx was admirably demonstrated in the South Atlantic, and it must remain an effective threat to surface vessels, well away from its parent ship. The Seaspray/Sea Skua system fitted to Lynx is shown in Fig. 3.18.

Troop Lift and Rescue Roles

Naval helicopters are also used for troop lifts, especially of Marines, stores lifts and liaison sorties, and special mention must be made of the search and rescue (SAR) role conducted in Britain both by the RN and the RAF. SAR helicopters have saved numerous lives off our coastlines in peacetime and have also been responsible for the recovery of space crews in the USA and aircraft crews. In

FIG. 3.18 Sea Lynx with Sea Skua

wartime, downed crews would continue to be rescued from the sea in the same way that earned such admiration during the last war. This role is frequently carried out in appalling conditions and often involves precision flying of a very high order. The electronics equipment and flight control systems carried by these aircraft must be capable of assisting the pilot to cope with such conditions, and these will be covered in later chapters. This is certainly one of the most humane roles carried out by helicopters, and Fig. 3.19 shows a typical rescue of a man from the sea by a Sea King helicopter.

FIG. 3.19 A typical SAR operation

SELF TEST QUESTIONS

QUESTION 1   What are the main roles of Army helicopters?

Answer a.   ....

        b.   ....

        c.   ....

        d.   ....

        e.   ....

QUESTION 2   What is the main advantage of roof- or mast-mounted sights?

Answer ....

....

....

QUESTION 3   How is television best used as an observation service?

Answer ....

....

....

QUESTION 4   Which countries have produced attack helicopters and what are they called?

Answer ....

....

....

....

QUESTION 5   Why have the USSR developed large, load-carrying helicopters?

Answer ....

....

....

QUESTION 6   What are the main roles of naval helicopters?

Answer ....

....

....

Answers on page 134

4.

Power Plants and Transmissions

Introduction

The value of the military helicopter today is due in no small measure to its ability to carry a useful payload over a good range. For a given design, this depends on the efficiency of the engine which should have a good power-to-weight ratio coupled with a low specific fuel consumption. Except for very small helicopters, which are no longer widely used by military forces, the gas turbine engine is used exclusively. In this chapter, therefore, much of the text will deal with the particular gas turbine type that is so widely used. In addition, a minor section will explain how the power output of the engine is transmitted to the rotors. Before dealing with these matters in detail, however, it will be helpful to describe briefly the background to the emergence of the gas turbine engine and how it works.

The Gas Turbine Engine

The earliest helicopters were fitted with reciprocating, petrol engines because these were highly developed and they offered a fair power-to-weight ratio, a good specific fuel consumption, good reliability and were readily available in various sizes. As the need for increased power became evident, petrol engines became increasingly complex multi-cylinder designs, their weight tended to increase and reliability became worse. Meanwhile, early gas turbine engines were becoming more efficient, but not yet as efficient as the best petrol engines, more reliable, and, most important of all, were able to provide very much higher power-to-weight and power-to-volume ratios. This was particularly so of the free turbine which dispensed with the need for a clutch in the transmission system; this is a draw-back in all reciprocating engines. The gas turbine thus became the most important engine employed in helicopter propulsion.

Configurations

The gas turbine is also widely used in fixed-wing aircraft. In this application it is usually a turbojet or a turbofan, which generates a high-speed jet to propel the aircraft forward at high subsonic or supersonic speeds. In helicopters, however, the gas turbine is not used as a means of producing a high-velocity jet but to produce power in the form of a rotating output shaft. This is connected to the

helicopter rotors through a mechanical transmission system and is known as a
turboshaft engine. It is a close relation of the fourth and final variant, the
turboprop, widely used on modern propeller-driven fixed-wing aircraft.

Principles of Operation

The principal function of any engine, broadly speaking, is to convert heat into a
useful form of mechanical power. No engine is capable of carrying out this
conversion with an efficiency of 100%. However, engines can be built to perform
at what are regarded as good efficiencies, and the gas turbine is such an engine.

It is based on a sequence of continuous operations in which different processes
are successively carried out to produce useful power. The major components
which constitute the heart of the gas turbine, which is called the gas generator,
are shown diagrammatically in Fig. 4.1 in their relative working positions.

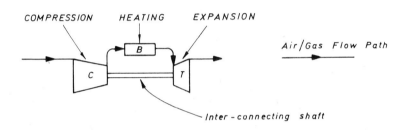

FIG. 4.1 Diagrammatic layout of a gas generator

What happens to the flow of gas when it leaves the turbine (T) determines
whether the engine is a turboshaft or a turbojet.

In Operation

In operation, the turbine receives high-pressure, hot gas (a mixture of air and
combustion products) which flows through the blades at high speed, causing the
turbine wheel to rotate. In so doing the energy content of the gas is depleted to
some extent. The energy extracted by the turbine wheel is transmitted through a
rotating central shaft to the aerodynamic compressor (C) upstream which
behaves in roughly the opposite manner to the turbine absorbing its output. The
compressor draws in atmospheric air, compresses it and directs it to the
combustor (B). Here, the air is mixed with fuel and burned to heat it to an
appropriate temperature before directing it to the turbine. The turbine then
allows the hot, high-pressure gas to expand through its blading, producing the
power to drive the compressor. These three components, the compressor, the
combustor and the turbine, form the gas generator.

In the case of the turbojet the partially expanded gas leaving the gas generator
flows directly to the propelling nozzle, as shown in Figs 4.2a and 4.2b.

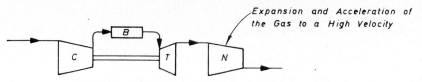

FIG. 4.2a Diagrammatic layout of a turbojet engine

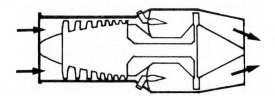

FIG. 4.2b Cross-section of a simple turbojet engine

This type of gas turbine produces a high-velocity jet of gas from the nozzle (N) as its useful output. This output is the propulsive force. Turbojet engines have been used on compound helicopters to provide additional forward speed. However, the turboshaft engine in which we are much more interested for helicopter application is shown in Figs 4.3a and 4.3b.

In this arrangement the gas producer, C + B + T1, behaves just as before. But immediately downstream of turbine T1 is another turbine T2. The T1 and T2 are known respectively as the high- and low-pressure turbines. Turbine T2, frequently mechanically separate from the gas generator section and may, therefore, rotate at a different speed, is now able to provide a direct drive to the load. The gas flowing through turbine T2 gives up most of its remaining energy to the turbine.

In the case of a helicopter the rotor is the load, being driven through a reduction gearbox. This is a typical turboshaft layout.

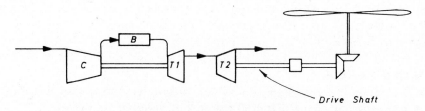

FIG. 4.3a Diagrammatic layout of a turboshaft engine

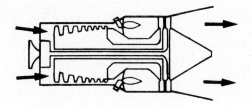

FIG. 4.3b Cross-section of a turboshaft engine

For completeness, variations on the two schemes described are illustrated in the cross-sections in Figs 4.4 and 4.5. The turbofan is a 'bypass' variant of the turbojet and the turboprop is a fixed-wing shaft power unit having many similarities to the turboshaft engine.

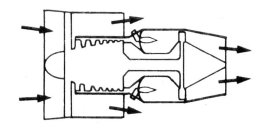

FIG. 4.4 Cross-section of a turbofan engine

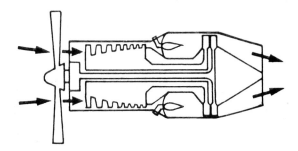

FIG. 4.5 Cross-section of a turboprop engine

Different Types of Turboshaft

There are two turboshaft configurations which are available. They are known as the free (power) turbine and the fixed turbine (or single shaft). There are several important distinctions between the two, both in their layout and application in helicopters.

The Fixed Turbine

A diagrammatic arrangement of a fixed turbine engine is shown in Fig. 4.6a and a cross-section of an actual fixed turbine engine in Fig. 4.6b.

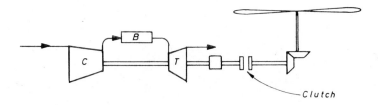

FIG. 4.6a Diagrammatic layout of a fixed turbine type

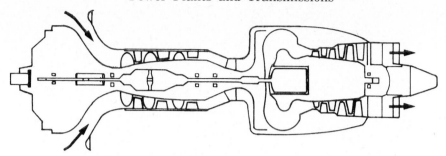

Fig. 4.6b Cross-section of a Turbomeca Astazou engine

The most important feature of this type of engine is that the output shaft, which feeds power to the gearbox and then to the rotor through a clutch, is directly connected to the single turbine. Thus there is a fixed relationship between the rotor rotational speed and the engine rotational speed. Since a helicopter rotor runs at approximately constant speed, the consequence is that the fixed turbine engine is constrained to operate at approximately constant rotational speed also. While this arrangement offers one or two advantages, such as a very rapid response to a load change imposed by an increase in rotor collective pitch, it also results in a rather inflexible engine. For example, since it is a constant speed engine it has to be rated at a rather modest power because of the need to sustain the chosen rotational speed. There is thus a built-in power limitation which prevents the achievement of high emergency powers even for short durations. In addition, the torque-speed characteristics of the engine are not well matched to the rotor. However, this problem can be largely dealt with by the provision of a suitable engine control system. There is also a weight penalty associated with the clutch and, finally, the specific fuel consumption at low or moderate powers is poor compared with that at the maximum power condition.

The main proponents of the fixed turbine type, Turbomeca in France, have built a series of such engines over a long period. Their particular design, shown in Fig. 4.6b, features the output shaft emerging from the compressor, or intake, end of the engine. This contrasts with the simpler design in Fig. 4.6a. Apart from the mechanical design arrangements, this particular layout is no different in principle from that shown in Fig. 4.6a. A subsequent section will include some remarks on the mechanical arrangements of engines for helicopters.

Free Turbine

We can now turn to the free turbine which is the most commonly used configuration in both single-engine and multi-engine helicopters. The main reason for the widespread adoption of this type is its favourable torque-speed characteristic, which is covered in more detail later in this chapter. It promotes rotor speed stability, reasonable specific fuel consumption at part-power operation, plus the simplicity resulting from the absence of a clutch in the output drive line. A diagrammatic layout of a free turbine engine is shown in Fig. 4.7a, with a cross-section of an actual free turbine engine in Fig. 4.7b.

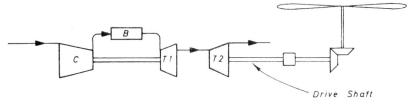

FIG. 4.7a Diagrammatic layout of a free turbine type

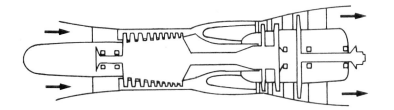

FIG. 4.7b Cross-section of a Rolls-Royce Gnome engine

The diagrammatic layout highlights the characteristic feature of the free turbine type, which is the absence of a mechanical connection between the gas generator (C + B + T1) and the output turbine (T2), which is thus free. In fact in a helicopter application the free turbine rotates at substantially constant speed under all conditions apart from transient states such as start-up and run-down. It is the gas generator which is free to operate over a range of speeds, to enable its gas flow to be best matched to the requirements of the power turbine. It should be noted that the power absorbed by the rotor can vary greatly according to operating conditions, despite the fact that the rotor speed is nominally constant. Thus the freedom presented by the ability of the gas generator section to run at different speeds as required is considerable.

However, the free turbine description really means no more than that the power turbine has a gas flow rather than mechanical link to the gas generator. The free turbine, therefore, behaves rather like a torque converter.

Component Detail

Apart from the distinction between the free turbine and the fixed turbine there are several other notable features which characterise certain designs.

Some engines have a wholly axial-flow compressor in which the air flows parallel to the axis of the shaft. Such a type is the Rolls-Royce Gnome engine shown in Fig. 4.7b. It has a multi-stage compressor and in order to obtain the desired flexible operating characteristics the first four rows of stators, which are fixed blades interspersed between the rotating compressor blades, have a mechanical arrangement to allow the blade angles to be altered. This ensures that the angle at which the flow of air meets the compressor blades is the most efficient. Such a device is a feature that would tend to be associated with first generation engines. Compression ratios of about 10:1 can be achieved by axial compressors.

An alternative approach is to adopt the Turbomeca pattern in which one or more axial-flow stages are succeeded by a centrifugal compressor which draws air in at the centre and forces it out at the outer edges by the action of the radiating vanes in a radial flow. The adoption of the centrifugal, or radial, stage tends to increase the engine cross-section, but this is not usually a serious disadvantage for a helicopter. Compression rates of around 4:1 are common with this type of compressor.

One way of obtaining a high-pressure ratio in the compressor is to adopt a multi-shaft approach as is done in the Rolls-Royce Gem engine shown in Fig. 4.8. In this free-turbine engine the gas generator itself has two coaxial shafts which run one inside the other. One is connected to the axial, and the other to the centrifugal compressor.

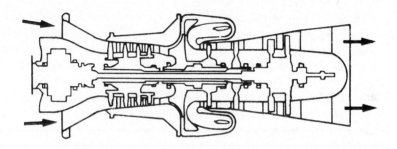

Fig. 4.8 Cross-section of a Rolls-Royce Gem engine

The four-stage axial-flow compressor lies upstream of the centrifugal compressor and each rotates at its best speed on its own shaft. The overall high pressure rise is thus obtained while preserving good handling characteristics without having to incorporate variable stator blades.

It follows that the two-shaft, or two-spool, gas generator of the Gem must have a high-pressure turbine on one shaft to drive the centrifugal compressor and a lower or intermediate pressure turbine on the other shaft to drive the axial compressor. Examination of the layout in Fig. 4.8 will confirm this. These two turbines are the axial-flow type, which is nearly always a feature of the gas turbine engine whether turboshaft or turbojet.

Another notable feature of the Gem engine is the reverse-flow combustor which is well matched to the radial-flow compressor immediately upstream of it. The adoption of this feature enables the designer to shorten the whole engine and so minimise mechanical problems which sometimes arise with long shafts.

The Gem is fairly unusual in that while it is of the free-turbine configuration, the output drive is taken through the gas generator out of the intake end. This has certain advantages in avoiding the output shaft passing through the wall of the exhaust and, in addition, may make siting of the engine on the helicopter, in relation to the rotor, much easier.

It should be noted that an engine may incorporate a reduction gearbox. High rotational speeds of gas turbines may lead to overall reduction ratios of the order of about 100:1 in some installations. Thus a gearbox giving part of the overall reduction may be part of the engine as supplied.

Finally, the concept of modular construction is important. This technique, in which a complete engine is designed as a collection of individual modules, such as, say, a compressor module, a free turbine module, or any other module, which can be assembled relatively easily, is said to result in a reduction in operational costs. The idea is that an unserviceable engine can be quickly repaired by exchanging the bad module for a good module. Otherwise the complete unserviceable engine would be withdrawn for overhaul. In this way, good modules are retained in service and fewer spare engines are required to sustain operations.

Special Helicopter Requirements

It need hardly be mentioned that ideally any aero-engine should have a low acquisition cost and a low operating cost. A high thermodynamic efficiency, which also means a high fuel efficiency, is important, as already indicated, and of course influences operating costs. Also desirable are high reliability and easy maintenance, both of which influence acquisition and operating costs.

However, there are several areas in which engine features special to helicopter operation are important. Perhaps the most important of these is the need for very rapid response to the pilot's demands. In particular when a pilot requires an unforeseen power increase to, say, combat adverse weather conditions on landing, he wants a rapid response from the engine. There are two sides to this requirement. Recognising that the power response characteristics of the free turbine configuration are inferior to those of the fixed turbine arrangement, because the former required the acceleration of the whole of the gas generator section, one manufacturer at least has developed a special governor to harness the superior characteristics of the fixed shaft engine, which, of course, is essentially a fixed-speed engine. The benefits of obtaining a power increase merely by raising turbine entry temperature rather than by the time-consuming spinning up of the gas generator to increase the gas through-flow are substantial. It is interesting to note that the Rolls-Royce Gem engine features a different approach to the problem of obtaining rapid response. The gas generator section of this free-turbine engine consists of two spools, which have contributed to the good response characteristics without going to the complication of variable stators.

Perhaps the second most important requirement is good part-load fuel economy. This is particularly so in the twin-engined helicopter whose engine size is designed to be able to meet an engine-out requirement. The consequence is that under normal cruising conditions each engine is operating at about 50% of its maximum rating. The gas turbine tends to be poor at part-loads and so an engine required for such an application would tend to be designed for a high pressure ratio and maximum cycle temperature that would afford a reasonable part-load economy. These features could result in adverse handling characteristics. However, it is true that the part-load fuel economy of the free turbine engine is superior to that of the fixed turbine engine, so multi-engine helicopters invariably use the free turbine type.

In addition to those important features already mentioned, there is also the need to be able to cope with intake air which has been contaminated by dirt or sand or exhaust gas. Depending on the siting of the engine(s) in relation to the main rotor gearbox, the intake air flow may be significantly disturbed. The ability to operate on contaminated fuel as well as a range of fuels is also important. Finally, the vibration environment presented in helicopter operation is very arduous and the structure of the engine thus tends to need to be very stiff.

The Transmission

The primary function of the transmission system is to transmit the drive provided by the engine to the rotor. In a single rotor helicopter there is a secondary function of providing drive to the anti-torque tail rotor.

It was noted before that some helicopter engines have an integral reduction gearbox. This means that a more manageable order of output in terms of revolutions per minute is provided. In all cases this rotational speed is much greater than the rotor requires and so further speed reducing must be provided. In addition, if we assume that, with few exceptions, the engines are positioned in the fuselage at right angles to the rotor mast, the transmission must turn the drive through this right angle. This dual function is accomplished in a bevel-type reduction gearbox.

Twin-engined helicopters need a gearbox which will accept two input drives to provide a single main output drive. This is a complex arrangement in which the power output of the two engines must be carefully matched. Such an installation is that in the Puma helicopter. The two Turbomeca Turbo engines provide the input at 23000 rev/min, while the single output to the rotor is reduced to 265 rev/min. This is an overall reduction ratio of about 100:1 which is not easily accomplished.

Quite apart from providing the proper speed reduction the main gearbox plus ancillaries should ideally be as light as possible, transmitting little vibration to the fuselage and offering reliable performance with a respectable overhaul time. Transmissions today are highly developed, much progress having been made since the days of the widespread use of the reciprocating engine. This has been achieved by raising allowable stress levels in gearing through better design and the use of better materials and manufacturing techniques. An advanced design of gearbox is that in the Westland WG30 helicopter. It is a shallow, low-maintenance, conformal design and is mounted on a vibration-absorbing raft along with two Gem engines, the whole raft itself being mounted on elastomeric suspension units. In this way, vibration is absorbed by this raft instead of being transmitted to the fuselage.

Future Technology

Priorities

Engine manufacturers continually striving to improve their product naturally concentrate on those aspects that require most attention. Of course, all aspects of engine performance could be improved, but the manufacturer has to balance, for example, the development time and cost against the improvement in, say, fuel consumption or reduction in weight or perhaps improving reliability. In the following paragraphs several aspects of technological improvements which are likely to be important in the next ten years or so are mentioned. It should be understood that the points discussed are not exhaustive and represent a personal view.

Reliability

One of the most significant areas requiring attention is that of reliability. All operators require the engine to perform as predicted and unscheduled interruptions are both inconvenient and costly. It may well be that a reduced emphasis on improved pure performance such as increased turbine entry temperature, component efficiency or reduced engine weight could be more than offset, in terms of cost of operation, by increasing the emphasis on improved component and system reliability and relatively unsophisticated engine features. This approach is not intended to inhibit the introduction of improved technological features, but is suggested as a means of pacing the introduction of innovations.

Improving Specific Fuel Consumption

Reliability is such an all-embracing aspect that it is almost impossible to mention other considerations which do not influence it. However, another requirement which will probably continue to challenge the engine manufacturer is the improvement of specific fuel consumption, particularly at cruise conditions when the twin-engined machine is running at a low percentage power. It may be that more highly optimised engine cycles will be adopted. A possible development for a long-range or long-endurance application is a recuperative engine similar to the Abrams tank engine. Such advances that do occur will have to take place while maintaining good handling qualities. No doubt, also, improvements in engine fuel management systems, possibly with a microelectronic base, will lead to improved response times, particularly in the free-turbine engine.

Engine Intake Protection

The helicopter frequently operates in a hostile environment in the sense that the engine ingests foreign matter such as dust, stones, ice and so on. Separating out stones, etc., and/or filtering pre-intake air are problems particular to the military helicopter. Engine intake protection in the form of particle separators may well be a standard feature in due course.

Infrared Suppression

For some years the suppression of infrared radiation from exhaust systems and exhaust gas has been actively pursued. It is anticipated that improved performance in this respect will be achieved over the next decade. The Black Hole Concept described in Chapter 7 has already gone some considerable way to resolve this problem by rapidly mixing ambient air with the engine efflux before it is exhausted to atmosphere.

Reduction of Weight

The application of composite materials is now quite common. It seems certain that their lightweight and low cost will ensure their increasing application, particularly where high temperatures do not occur. In engines in particular, ceramics show promise; however, it may be more than ten years hence before a production engine is available.

Reduction of Cost

Finally, in these days of strictly controlled budgets, perhaps the most important consideration of all is the cost of acquiring and operating helicopter engines. Of course the various technological points mentioned in the preceding paragraphs affect both costs. But since the operating cost for a normal life will exceed the cost of acquisition, it is thought that henceforth the manufacturer and operator will concentrate on developments such as improved reliability, maintainability, fuel control systems and environmental protection.

Improved performance in terms of reliability, cruise fuel consumption, power-to-weight ratio, handling and operating cost will assume increasing importance.

Military Helicopters
SELF TEST QUESTIONS

QUESTION 1   What type of engine is employed in most military helicopters?

Answer ....

QUESTION 2   What is probably its greatest virtue in helicopter installations?

Answer ....

....

QUESTION 3   Name the three fundamental components of a typical turbo-shaft engine.

Answer ....

....

....

QUESTION 4   Name the two distinct variants of gas-turbine engine employed in helicopters

Answer ....

....

QUESTION 5   Why does the output shaft of a helicopter engine have to rotate at substantially constant speed?

Answer ....

....

....

....

QUESTION 6   What component is required in the transmission of the Gazelle
               helicopter which is superfluous in the Lynx helicopter?

               Answer ....

               ....

               ....

               ....

QUESTION 7   Why is the free-turbine type of engine always employed in a
               multi-engine helicopter?

               Answer ....

               ....

               ....

QUESTION 8   What feature of construction in some of today's engines leads to
               improved availability?

               Answer ....

               ....

               ....

QUESTION 9   What is probably the most important power plant characteristic,
               from the pilot's point of view?

               Answer ....

               ....

QUESTION 10   How can infrared radiation from the engine be minimised?

               Answer ....

               ....

Answers on page 134

5.
Avionics

Introduction

Avionics is the general term which covers electrical and electronic devices for use in aviation; it refers especially to electronic control systems for aircraft and airborne weapons. From this definition it will be seen that it is a loose term capable of a wide range of interpretations and it is difficult to decide exactly where avionics start and finish. However, from the very broad range of equipments and devices involved, this chapter will concentrate on four of the more important: they are flight instruments, navigational aids, automatic flight control systems and future systems.

Flight Instruments

The Need

Early aviators flying at low level and only in good weather had little need for flight instruments. They relied on the abundance of visual clues and their own inherent feel for the aircraft to fly efficiently and successfully. However, when flying in thick cloud or fog, the three senses normally used by a pilot—vision, the inner ear and feel through the body—become ineffective or misleading. So aids to enable pilots to keep their aircraft safely in the air and then also to perform a safe landing were developed. Gyroscopes are widely used in flight instruments, utilising rigidity or gyroscopic inertia to assist the pilot select the correct attitude and maintain the appropriate heading. In the diagram of a standard instrument panel shown in Fig. 5.1, three of the instruments, the Artificial Horizon (AH), Directional Indicator (DI) and Turn and Slip Indicator (T/S), are all gyroscopic instruments. The remaining three instruments will be discussed later.

Artificial Horizon

The Artificial Horizon or Attitude Indicator gives a direct, continuous natural presentation of aircraft attitudes in pitch and roll. It is the most important flight instrument, at the heart of which is a gyroscope with an axis which is set horizontally. It will be appreciated that the case of the instrument, fixed to the air-frame, contains a fixed indicator on its face which moves in exactly the same way as the aircraft. Within the case, the gyroscope, spinning at several thousand revolutions per minute, has a horizontal bar, called the horizon bar, attached to it; this remains horizontal when flying. The aircraft and, therefore, the fixed

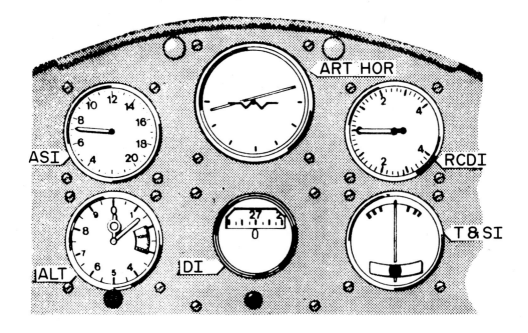

FIG. 5.1 Standard instrument panel

indicator move relative to the horizon bar in flight and it is the difference between the indicator and the bar which tells the pilot what the attitude of his aircraft is at any time. A typical AH presentation is shown at Fig. 5.2 and three different conditions of flight are shown at Fig. 5.3.

Turn and Slip Indicators

The turn and slip indicator shows movement of the aircraft in the yawing (i.e. about the vertical axis) and the rolling planes. It consists of two separate instruments in one case. The turn indicator employs a rate gyro which is shown in simple form in Fig. 5.4. It uses the second important characteristic of gyroscopes, precession, to indicate a rate of turn. On the diagram, if the base of the gyroscope turns in the direction of the arrow, as the aircraft turns to the left, a force is applied in the direction of arrow A. Precession causes the force to act at 90° in the direction of rotation, which means that the resultant force will be felt in direction of arrow B. This will cause the pointer on the scale to move to the left, to indicate a rate of turn. In British instruments, the scale normally reads from 1 to 4 each side of the zero mark. A rate one turn is equal to turning 3° per second, rate two 6° per second and so on. Turn and slip indicators can be incorporated into the Artificial Horizon in modern aircraft.

FIG. 5.2 A typical artificial horizon

(b) Level turn to right (c) Level steep climb

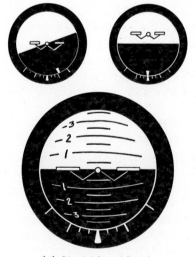

(a) Straight and level

FIG. 5.3 How the AH indicates different flight conditions

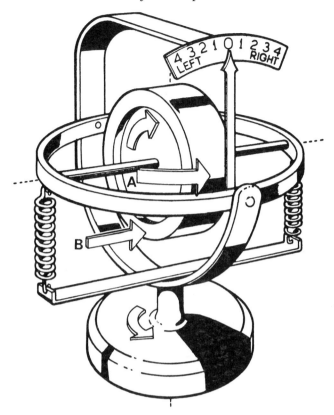

FIG. 5.4 A rate gyro used in a turn indicator

When executing a turn it is easy either to slip inwards towards the centre of the turn or to slide outwards away from the turn. The slip indicator is a relatively simple device which indicates either state to the pilot. It is based either on a pendulous weight system or is simply a ball-in-tube inclinometer which indicates lateral level during straight and level flight or slip and skid in a turn.

Directional Indicator (DI)

The Directional Indicator contains a gyroscope which rotates at a high speed in the region of 10,000–20,000 rpm about a horizontal axis. It provides a stable reference in azimuth for accurate course steering and precise turning. Since it is non-magnetic, it must be set with reference to a magnetic compass and it is not subject to normal compass errors. A more modern version called the gyromagnetic compass combines the advantages of gyroscopic stabilisation which is related at all times to the earth's magnetic meridian. Figure 5.5 shows a typical Direction Indicator.

The gyroscopes in all these instruments can be driven by electrical means or by high-pressure air acting on the outer rim of the rotating mass.

FIG. 5.5 A Direction Indicator

Pressure Operated Instruments

Having dealt with the three gyroscopic instruments, we now move on to the other three instruments on the standard panel which are pressure-operated flight instruments. They are the altimeter (ALT), the airspeed indicator (ASI) and the vertical speed indicator (VSI). All three instruments are supplied with air pressure by a method known as the pitot static system through a device known as the pressure head. It is situated below the nose of the helicopter as shown in Fig. 5.6.

FIG. 5.6 Pressure or pitot head

The function of the pressure head is to supply information about atmospheric pressure conditions outside the aircraft to the pressure-operated instruments. It is designed to transmit dynamic pressure caused by the forward movement of the aircraft through the air and can also transmit static pressure, which is air at normal ambient pressure. Sometimes static pressure is fed to the instruments through special static vents. Figure 5.7 shows a diagram of a pressure system which transmits both dynamic and static pressure to the instruments.

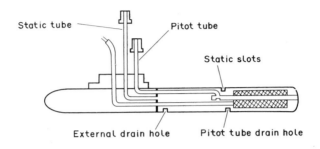

FIG. 5.7 A pitot/static pressure system

Altimeter

The pressure altimeter is simply an aneroid barometer which measures atmospheric pressure. In a basic altimeter, an air-tight case containing a partially evacuated aneroid capsule is connected to the static pressure system. A leaf spring prevents the capsule from collapsing under the surrounding atmospheric pressure. As the aircraft climbs or descends, the change in pressure around the capsule causes it to expand or contract. This movement is magnified by a system of levers to a pointer on a dial graduated in height. A baroscale is also normally built into the instrument with a knob for setting a pressure reading on the scale. When an airfield pressure called the QFE is set, the pointer will be at zero when on the ground at the airfield in question. If mean sea level pressure, QNH, is set, the instrument will indicate height above mean sea level. An altimeter showing the baroscale and adjusting knob is shown in Fig. 5.8. The pressure altimeter is being supplemented or replaced by radar altimeters in modern aircraft. This instrument uses radar principles to give a very accurate indication of altitude.

Airspeed Indicator

The airspeed indicator measures the speed of a helicopter relative to the air. It consists of an airtight case divided into two parts by a flexible diaphragm. One chamber is connected to the static tube, the other to the pitot tube. At rest, equal pressure in both chambers causes the diaphragm to be at rest. In flight, dynamic pressure through the pitot tube causes the diaphragm to distend in direct proportion to it. This movement is fed through a system of levers on to a dial calibrated in knots. Many airspeed indicators contain a capsule in place of the diaphragm. It operates in exactly the same way: static and dynamic pressure are fed inside it with only static pressure surrounding it.

Fig. 5.8 A pressure altimeter

Vertical Speed Indicator (VSI)

The vertical speed indicator shows rate of climb and descent. It is a much more sensitive instrument than the altimeter and is a valuable aid for descending through cloud and landing in poor visibility. It consists of a sensitive metal capsule inside an airtight case. The capsule is fed static pressure and this is also fed to the inside of the case through a metering unit, which restricts the rate of flow. It is the resulting differential between the air pressure inside the capsule and that surrounding it which is measured. If the aircraft climbs or descends at a constant rate, for example, the metering unit will maintain the differential pressure corresponding to that rate. Since both temperature and pressure changes in the atmosphere could cause false readings, VSIs contain mechanical devices to compensate for both. A diagram of a simple VSI is shown in Fig. 5.9.

Limitations to the Use of Instruments

The six instruments which have been described form a basic package of instruments which the pilot requires to fly and land safely in poor weather and bad visibility conditions. They have been described in their simplest form. Other more sophisticated instruments can combine many functions, but they are outside the scope of this chapter. Figure 5.10 shows the layout of a Westland Lynx flight instrument panel, which is currently in service.

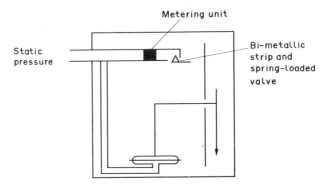

Fig. 5.9 A simple VSI

Fig. 5.10 Lynx flight instruments

Instrument Landing System

Even with such a pack of flight instruments, a pilot is still unable to land his machine when in cloud unless he is talked down by an Air Traffic Controller. To overcome this deficiency, an Instrument Landing System (ILS) has been devised. Three radio beams inform the pilot of his angle of descent (glideslope), his alignment with the runway (localiser) and his distance from touchdown over two markers. This information is displayed on an instrument which can be seen in Fig. 5.11.

FIG. 5.11 An ILS instrument

If both cross-bars on the instrument are kept central, the aircraft will fly down a 2.5° glideslope to the end of the runway. Even so, the pilot must be able to see the ground before touching down and a cloud base of about 200 feet above ground level is normally the minimum acceptable. Battlefield helicopters can utilise a similar technique using a mobile, automatic ground beacon both as a navigation and landing aid in bad weather. However, modern target acquisition techniques such as thermal imaging, which can see through bad weather, are making such systems unnecessary for battlefield use, and they have the added attraction of being self-contained.

Navigational Aids

The Need

Most peacetime navigational aids depend on a form of ground network to provide information to equipment carried on the aircraft. Clearly, a battlefield helicopter cannot rely on such external sources during a war, so a form of self-contained system is essential. In its most basic form this consists of a pilot using a map; consequently navigation and map reading techniques are still taught and widely used by most aviators. However, the introduction of increasingly sophisticated equipment, plus the need to operate at very low level, overloaded the crew to such an extent that assistance in position fixing and navigation had to be introduced. There are two types of self-contained systems currently available, Doppler systems and inertial systems. The former is in general use in many battlefield helicopters.

Doppler Systems

The Doppler effect has been described fully in the Introductory Volume and in Volume VII. The principles involved are generally well known. In a helicopter navigation system the ground speed of the machine is deduced by directing a narrow beam of energy on to the ground ahead and measuring the frequency difference between the transmitted wave and the reflected wave. These differences are independent of the distance to the reflecting surface, so height above ground and rough terrain do not affect the accuracy of the system. In a similar way drift can be deduced.

One to four beams can be used to measure speed and drift in what is commonly called the Janus system, from the two-faced Roman god who was able to look forwards and backwards simultaneously.

The Decca Tactical Air Navigation System (TANS), which is installed in the Westland Lynx, consists of a computer which is fed by a Doppler radar, compass, vertical reference gyroscope and True Airspeed (TAS) sensors. The function of the TAS sensors is to act as a back-up should the radar fail.

From the information it receives, the computer can calculate fourteen different functions, of which the most important are present position in grid or latitude and longitude, and position plus bearing and distance to any one of ten different points. Heading and range to intercept any of ten targets moving on a fixed course and speed which have been fed into the computer, called a moving waypoint, can also be computed. This function is more important to the naval variant of Lynx. Aircrew access is through a keyboard, and information from the computer can be displayed in alpha-numeric form on an indicator in the unit, or a further output can drive a moving cursor on a roller map, with a degree of accuracy of 2% of distance flown, or better. The TANS computer display is shown in Fig. 5.12.

While Doppler systems are not passive, the beams are directional and are directed downwards at angles of 60° or more with the horizontal. At the heights at which battlefield helicopters are expected to fly, there is little danger of interceptions by the enemy, except in the rare event of overflying on radar intercept. Doppler systems could, however, be susceptible to jamming. Inertial navigation is immune to jamming and meteorological conditions, and is passive; it could well assume greater importance in the future.

Automatic Flight Control Systems (AFCS)

Role

The term automatic flight control systems has been used to describe many different types of device for providing automatic control of an aircraft's flight path. This section deals with broad principles as they are applied to helicopters: there are marked differences between these and fixed-wing aircraft systems.

FIG. 5.12 TANS computer

An AFCS is employed to permit a pilot to perform a task more accurately or more easily, to enable him to perform a task which the helicopter would otherwise be unable to do, or to relieve him of a flying task altogether. Since an AFCS has a shorter response time and gives more accurate control than a pilot, the helicopter flies more accurately, is more stable, essential when firing weapons, and allows the pilot to concentrate on other more important operational tasks.

Autostabilisers and Autopilots

The type of AFCS in current use has two parts, an autostabiliser and an autopilot. The autostabiliser relieves the pilot of the immediate second-to-second control of the aircraft. Unlike fixed-wing aircraft, the helicopter is basically unstable and so a system which will improve its stability while still allowing the pilot to use the controls manually is of great benefit. Essentially, the autostabiliser is a damping device in pitch and roll as well as damping out turbulence, without the authority to hold a given datum; it is frequently referred to as a Stabilised Augmentation System (SAS). A simple autostabiliser uses information from a rate gyroscope which operates through series actuators to provide rate damping. It will not try to turn the helicopter to a given attitude, but will merely reduce the rate of change to zero.

The autopilot, on the other hand, actually flies the aircraft instead of the pilot. It can memorise one or all of heading, height and airspeed. A magnetically monitored gyrocompass system is normally used to produce a heading input, although radio navigation systems may also be used. The height and airspeed inputs are provided from capsules similar to those used in altimeters and ASIs which have been specially adapted to give the appropriate electrical signals; radar altimeter height and radar speed signals may also be used. Most autopilots have a trim facility for adjusting the data after selection, as shown in Fig 5.13.

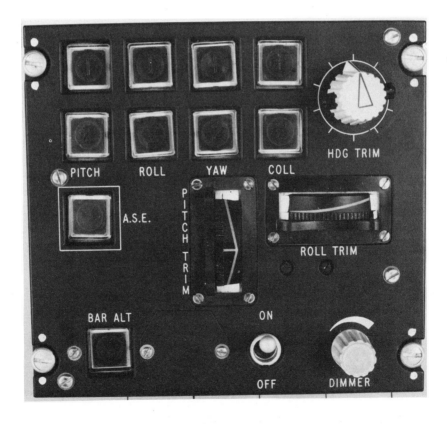

FIG. 5.13 AFCS trimmers in a Westland Lynx

In order to assist him to fly the aircraft the pilot will switch in his autostabiliser and he may then allow his autopilot to perform all the flying functions for him while he performs more important tasks. The pilot has the ability to override the autopilot at all times in the event of a system runaway or failure.

Future Systems

Data Bus and Electronic Display

Each of the vital components in a helicopter, such as gearboxes, engines, etc., has to be monitored for temperatures and pressures, and this information passed to instruments in the cockpit. The sensors involved each have a dedicated pair of wires which run along the fuselage to the back of the appropriate instrument. It is now possible, using microprocessors, to do away with these discrete wires by running only one pair of wires round the aircraft joining sensor to sensor, then to the control panel. Each sensor can be interrogated in turn, its output information computed and this can then be presented in an easily understood format on a video display unit at the push of a button. The data bus saves weight, improves reliability and enables the pilot to monitor his sensors as he requires them. He is no longer confronted with a mass of information which largely only confirms that all is well. The system can be engineered to flash on to the screen any system which looks like going wrong or has suddenly failed, without being interrogated.

The US Mil Std-1553 data bus is already in service and is likely to be improved quite soon by introducing fibre optics. By dispensing with the spaghetti-like mass of wires, the 1553B version offers many advantages, not least that it is fast becoming accepted internationally as a standard. The advent of fibre optic data buses and very high-speed integrated circuits, or very high-performance integrated circuits, will dramatically increase the ability to process data and help realise the enormous potential for automation to relieve the crew of many cockpit management tasks.

Direct Voice Input (DVI)

The next logical step is to remove the need for push-button interrogation by using a computer which recognises voice patterns and then causes the appropriate information to appear on the video screen. Thus before starting a sortie, a pilot will be required to say, for example, key words a number of times to confirm his voice pattern to the computer. During his sortie, when he needs the flight instruments on display, he will simply say the appropriate key word. The presentation he wants will then automatically appear. This applies to flight information, engine performance, weapon state and navigation information. It should also be possible to select a radio frequency automatically, simply by stating the frequency and also to call up a pictorial map presentation by saying the appropriate word. This type of system is under development now and could well come into service with the next generation of helicopters.

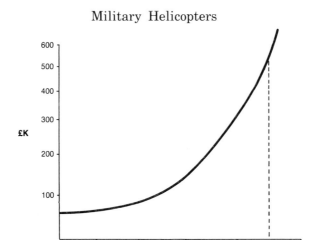

£K

% of year flyable

FIG. 5.14 The cost of avionics

Advanced Flight Controls

In addition to fly-by-wire/light mentioned in later chapters, a new control system is under development in the USA. This consists of a small, single hand grip called a sidearm control, which will replace all three conventional controls currently in use. The single control, stationed at waist height, at the pilot's right hand, will be just a few inches high. It will be fixed, but when pressure is applied it will act in the same natural sense as conventional controls, to move the aircraft in the same direction as the pressure being applied. Vertical flight will be achieved by applying pressure up and down and yaw will be controlled by twisting it. Although this sounds complex, it should be a fairly easy matter to master such a control. Coupled with a data bus, electronic display and DVI, it will make life very much easier for the pilot. But this will inevitably be a costly business, and avionics is already a very expensive part of a helicopter's total equipment. The more that is required of the helicopter in terms of operating at very low level in bad weather and at night, the more comprehensive becomes its avionics fit and the more expensive the aircraft as a whole. Figure 5.14 shows how the cost of operating in bad conditions escalates dramatically above about 60%. The value of being able to operate up to 90% of the time can only be calculated by the planners, but it would clearly be unwise to hamstring an otherwise very effective weapons system by denying it the ability to operate in the very conditions which are likely to be exploited by an enemy.

SELF TEST QUESTIONS

QUESTION 1   What is meant by 'avionics'?

Answer ....

....

....

QUESTION 2   Which gyroscopic instruments appear on the instrument panels
of most modern helicopters?

Answer ....

....

....

QUESTION 3   What information does an Instrument Landing System provide?

Answer ....

....

....

QUESTION 4   How many types of self-contained navigational aid are currently
available and what are they?

Answer ....

....

QUESTION 5   What is the function of an autostabiliser?

Answer ....

....

....

Answers on page 135

QUESTION 6 What is the function of an autopilot?

Answer ....

....

....

QUESTION 7 What is a data bus?

Answer ....

....

....

QUESTION 8 How does Direct Voice Input work?

Answer ....

....

....

QUESTION 9 What is a sidearm control?

Answer ....

....

....

6.

The Helicopter as a Weapons Platform

Introduction

The potential of a weapons platform that can respond quickly and move very rapidly about the battlefield unhindered by obstacles without being tied to conventional routes has not been lost upon modern armies. The earliest attempts to take advantage of the helicopters inherent capabilities resulted in MG being fitted to early types. Figure 6.1 shows a 0.30 calibre MG fitted to a French Alouette.

FIG. 6.1 0.30 calibre MGs fitted to an Alouette

Indeed, the French Army was one of the first to appreciate the value of such mobile firepower, which they put to good use in their campaign in Algeria. It was

79

from such humble beginnings that modern-day attack and armed helicopters have developed.

Machine Guns and Cannon

It was inevitable that the early attempts to arm helicopters, using airframes already in service performing other roles, should involve buttoning onto them weapons which were also in service. It was also inevitable that the resulting weapons system was not ideal, even though it could make a significant contribution to a battle. For example, the only way to aim a fixed forward firing MG at a target is to aim the whole aircraft at the target before opening fire, which is acceptable in a high-speed fighter aircraft but far from ideal in a helicopter. The fact that the helicopter is basically unstable and is constantly twitching when in a hover makes firing in a dive, when the aircraft's stability is increased by its forward speed, more accurate. However, by adopting this method of attack the helicopter is constantly reducing the range between itself and the target and bringing itself within range of similar ground weapons, probably mounted on more stable platforms. Add to this serious drawback the fact that the crew could not actually get at the weapon should there be a stoppage in flight, plus the elaborate ammunition chutes needed to guide ammunition from inside the fuselage to the weapon, and it is easy to see why this system has not enjoyed widespread popularity.

An alternative solution is to mount MG or cannon on pintles on the cabin floor. To take the weight of the weapon plus its mount and to absorb the recoil forces, it is necessary to strengthen the floor, and it can be seen from Fig. 6.2 that such installations can be cumbersome and heavy.

Again, complicated ammunition feeds are required to serve the weapon, and a collector or system of ejection is necessary to remove the empty cases. When firing such weapons, the gunner must make an allowance for the forward speed of the helicopter and, using a high percentage of tracer ammunition, must hose the stream of fire onto his target. Clearly, this is very expensive on ammunition and, at best, can only be described as an area weapon, since it is inherently so inaccurate. In addition and to be as effective as possible, a weapon should be mounted on both sides of the cabin so that the aircraft does not have to manoeuvre to bring fire to bear. This increases the payload involved significantly because two sets of everything are needed, including the gunner, and so the helicopter's endurance is reduced markedly. Even so, the pintle mounted system is still in use today on some armed helicopters and to provide a form of self-protection for utility and transport helicopters.

A grave disadvantage suffered by both MG and cannon is that they are relatively short-range weapons. To close to firing range, therefore, could well bring an aircraft too near the enemy and leave it open to retaliatory fire from the target or from other unseen targets in the immediate vicinity. This drawback has not prevented various armies equipping their helicopters with MG or cannon, which, with certain enhancements, can still be potent weapons, as we shall see later.

FIG. 6.2 0.5 inch MG mounted on a Westland Scout helicopter

Free Flight Rockets

Another cheap and relatively simple way of increasing the firepower of a helicopter, is to fit it with free flight rockets. These can be longer range than an MG or cannon and can deliver a greater weight of fire in a shorter time on to the target. This type of weapon is essentially an area weapon, even though recent improvements to rocket motors have improved their accuracy. The only sensible way to mount rockets on a helicopter is to attach pods on to stub wings or hard points on the fuselage, which means that they also can only be used in a fixed forward-firing configuration. There is little recoil to be absorbed. Although rockets appear to be very attractive, a reasonable degree of accuracy is best achieved when flying toward the target in stable flight, which again brings the helicopter closer to the enemy during the firing phase. The pilot can turn away immediately after firing, leaving the rockets to follow a ballistic trajectory to the target. This type of weapon is popular in the USA and USSR, both of whom have equipped both armed and attack helicopters with a combination of missiles, rockets, guns and cannon. Figure 6.3 shows the Huey Cobra weapon stations, including two 19-shot rocket pods of which 15 have been fired from each pod.

FIG. 6.3 Huey Cobra showing two partly expended rocket pods

Anti-tank Guided Missiles

Command to Line-of-sight (CLOS) Missiles

Clearly, the best weapon for a helicopter is one which can be used from maximum stand-off ranges while exposing the machine to the enemy for the shortest possible time; it should be recoilless, enable the helicopter to manoeuvre during the firing sequence and be cost-effective in contributing to the land battle. The anti-tank guided weapon meets most of these requirements and, since AFVs pose a major threat on the modern battlefield, can provide commanders with a valuable adjunct to ground-based and other aerial systems.

Early missiles available were of the command to line-of-sight type (CLOS) and Fig. 6.4 shows an SS11 CLOS missile being fired from a Westland Scout helicopter, in service for many years with the British Army Air Corps.

FIG. 6.4 An SS11 missile fired from a Westland Scout AH Mk1

These missiles are fired and controlled by an airgunner using an Avimo Ferranti (AF 120) roof-mounted sight, which is used both to acquire and identify the target, then to gather the missile before guiding it home. To do this, at least two different magnifications are required in the sight optics, and the AF 120 has $\times 2\frac{1}{2}$ for acquisition and missile gathering and $\times 10$ for target identification and the final guidance stage. Higher orders of magnification are now common in more modern sights. In the sight, the airgunner sees a spot of light produced by an IR flare in the base of the missile, and he controls this using a miniature joystick; it transmits control changes to the missile along a pair of wires. Such first-generation missiles are slow, with a time of flight of about 20 seconds to 3000 metres, which requires the aircraft to hover, partially exposed, for too long. Controlling this type of missile is difficult and demands a high standard of training for the gunner, and the need was quickly identified for a faster missile which would also be easier to control.

Semi-automatic Command to Line-of-sight Missiles
In both the USA and Europe, semi-automatic command to line-of-sight (SACLOS) systems have been developed which merely require the gunner to keep the sight's cross-hairs aligned on the target. An on-board computer senses any deviation of the missile away from this datum and automatically passes corrections to the missile, again down a pair of wires. The US TOW missile is such a semi-automatic system, which proved its worth in Vietnam, achieving an 82% hit rate against various types of target. Wire guidance has been a popular method in the Western world until recently, and certain Soviet missiles use the same technique, although their Swatter missile uses radio guidance. Clearly radio guidance is more susceptible to jamming, although radio guided missiles can be faster than wire guided, because they have no wires to dispense. One further disadvantage of a wire guided missile is that a device must be carried to sever the wires after impact at the target; discarded wires can be a hazard to a helicopter which hovers over them and sweeps them into the rotor disc or tail rotor.

The Attack Helicopter

Origins

It was in Vietnam that the helicopter truly came of age. They were used extensively by the American Army, and it was here also that the helicopter gunship proved itself a viable weapon of war. The armed utility helicopter, such as the UH-1 series shown in Fig. 6.5, equipped with a variety of weapons, gave sterling service and it was here that the world's first dedicated attack helicopter, the Huey Cobra, appeared. This purpose-built helicopter is still in service today and it can carry a combination of rockets, cannon, MG, automatic grenade launcher and TOW missiles. The weapon stations are shown in Fig. 6.6.

Sighting Developments

It will be noted that an additional mounting for the MG or grenade launcher has been devised in the form of a chin-mounted turret. This weapon is slaved to the gunner's sight and to an eyepiece on the pilot's helmet. It enables him to engage a target either by sighting it through the nose-mounted sight or through the eyepiece, then opening fire. The gun or grenade launcher is automatically slaved on to the target, the lead angle computed and effective fire delivered on to the target. The benefits to the crew in being able to control a slaved weapon instinctively are great, both in terms of flight safety and survivability. It will be no surprise that a similar but improved device called the Integrated Helmet and Display Sight System (IHADSS) will enter service with the USA's second-generation attack helicopter.

FIG. 6.5 UH-1 armed with rockets and MG

Fig. 6.6 Huey Cobras weapon stations

It will also be noted that the Americans have developed a sight which is mounted in the nose of the Cobra rather than in the roof, which is the preference of European armies. A nose or chin sight necessitates more of the helicopter being exposed in the frontal arc when firing from the hover, but this is offset to some extent by the very narrow fuselage, achieved by the tandem seating arrangement for the crew. The USA's second-generation attack helicopter, the Apache, retains the nose-mounted sight, although this is combined with various sensors for the gunner and the pilot as will be shown later.

Armed or Attack Helicopters?

Having established that it is possible to mount weapons on helicopters and for such a weapons system to make a useful contribution on the battlefield, the decision has to be made as to whether the aircraft is to be a dedicated attack helicopter or not. Utility helicopters with button-on weapons can perform a number of other tasks such as casualty evacuation or troop lifts, before being committed to armed action. The dedicated attack helicopter, on the other hand, is such a specialised machine that it cannot perform anything other than its primary fighting role. Clearly, although the armed helicopter offers more flexibility, the attack helicopter is expected to function in a very hostile environment, and must, therefore, be designed to survive. The choice boils down to a question of finance. Those nations able to afford attack helicopters plus the additional utility helicopters needed to perform other tasks have not hesitated to procure them. Those with a more restricted budget have been forced to accept the armed variant as a general workhorse. That is not to say that the armed variant will not make a significant contribution to a battle. The Westland Lynx equipped with TOW missiles, shown in Fig. 6.7, is capable of destroying large numbers of tanks which have penetrated forward positions. The ratio of helicopter-to-tank losses is at least 1:10 according to recent trials and exercises, with the Russians suggesting that 19 tanks killed per helicopter lost is probably realistic.

FIG. 6.7 A Westland Lynx equipped with TOW missiles

Similarly, the French and German armies have armed a proportion of their Gazelle and Bo 105 fleets with HOT missiles in the anti-tank role, and the Italians are trialling HOT on their Agusta A109. The Bo 105/HOT system is shown in Fig. 6.8. The US Defender 500 MD and Blackhawk UH-60 both have a considerable armed capability.

Despite the flexibility offered by armed helicopters, most nations now recognise the need for a specialised attack helicopter which is better fitted to fight and survive in the forward battle zone. The ability of such aircraft to penetrate the FEBA and attack enemy formations in the flank or from the rear is a valuable attribute and they are likely to make a far greater direct contribution in battle than an armed helicopter which is restricted to counter-penetration tasks. Attack helicopters could, for example, greatly assist armoured formations in a breakout phase by judicious use of shock action where it is least expected. The two nations who have shown the greatest interest in attack helicopters and their employment are those which can afford them, the USSR and the USA. It is, therefore, inevitable that as leaders in the field they have each produced a superb example of an attack helicopter, the Hind and Apache respectively.

The MI-24 Hind

The Soviet Union have long favoured helicopter operations in strength and were quick to arm their utility helicopters to provide firepower for heliborne attacks. The Hoplite and Hip helicopters were equipped with MG. rockets and

ATGW, and Hip, the most heavily armed, can also carry a 12.7 mm chin-mounted MG, four Swatter missiles plus 192 rockets in six pods. In the early 1970s the Hind A appeared. This was not strictly a dedicated attack helicopter as we know it but more of a well-armed, large, troop-carrying aircraft. Following their philosophy of evolutionary development, the Soviets produced several marks of Hind, the D and E series being noticeably in the attack mould. Figure 6.9 shows the most recent variant, a Hind F, with the weapons stations and sensor package under the nose being clearly visible.

FIG. 6.8 Bo 105 armed with HOT missiles

What the Soviets have produced is a large, fast helicopter which has many interesting features.

Engines

Two turboshaft TV3-117 engines are mounted on top of the fuselage, each capable of developing 1650 kW. These are powerful engines which operate well below maximum power in normal flight. This means that the exhaust temperatures are comparatively low, producing a small IR signature.

Weapons

A 12.7 mm multi-barrelled gun is mounted in a chin turret with a range of about 1300 m and an estimated rate of fire of around 4000 rounds/minute. 2000 rounds of ammunition are carried for this gun, which will be effective in both the air-to-ground and air-to-air roles. In addition, 128 × 57 mm rockets are carried in four pods and there are four launch rails for Swatter or Spiral anti-tank missiles. Bombs can also be carried on the weapon pylons, which appears compatible with the intention of the Soviets to use this helicopter in a close support role when FGA may not be available because of bad weather. The stub wings which carry the rockets and ATGW also have an aerodynamic function in forward flight: they offload the main rotor by about 25%, which improves the aircraft's manoeuvrability.

Fig. 6.9 Soviet Hind F

Avionics

A good surveillance and target acquisition fit is important in working towards day and night operations in bad weather. In the two pods beneath the nose of Hind are low-light TV or an IR device for target acquisition and tracking, a laser range-finder and a goniometer for missile tracking and, in the smaller of the two pods, a missile command link and possibly radar for target acquisition. A short-range navigation aid and a threat warning system are also carried.

Protection

Both crew compartments are protected by armour, as are the ammunition bay and fuel tanks. The latter are also self-sealing. Ballistic tolerance is generally good, although there have been some losses in Afghanistan to heavy MG/cannon fire.

The AH-64A Apache

Encouraged by the success of the Huey Cobra series, and following a policy of aggressive use of battlefield helicopters, it was inevitable that the United States should produce a second-generation attack helicopter. The Apache is designed primarily to operate by day and night in adverse weather against armour. It is a rugged machine, built to survive and operate from forward areas, and it will be seen from Fig. 6.10 that it also has many novel advanced features.

FIG. 6.10 AH-64 Apache

Weapons

A mix of rockets and Hellfire missiles can be carried in addition to the Hughes 30 mm Chain Gun, which is suspended beneath the fuselage on a collapsible mount. Up to sixteen Hellfire laser guided missiles can be combined with 1200 rounds of 30 mm ammunition, or a combination of missiles and rockets, but always with the Chain Gun, which is a permanent fixture. These weapons give the aircraft a very considerable air-to-ground and air-to-air capability. Figure 6.11 shows the weapons which Apache can carry.

TADS/PNVS

The Target Acquisition and Designation Sight (TADS) plus the Pilot's Night Vision Sensor (PNVS) mounted in the nose of the helicopter represent a major advance in night and adverse weather operations. TADS is the gunner's aid and contains direct view optics (DVO), forward looking IR (FLIR), TV, a laser designator/range-finder and a laser tracker. The pilot's aid, PNVS, is also a FLIR device. This package of sensors is significantly better than any other system currently in service and should allow the aircraft to operate for about 90% of all flying conditions, but it is expensive. However, it is felt that the high cost of enabling the aircraft to operate in all but the worst weather is justified, since enemy armour is likely to utilise those very conditions which make flying difficult.

Fig. 6.11 Apache's weapons

Performance

The Apache is powered by two T700-GE-701 General Electric turboshaft
engines, each rated at 1690 shaft horsepower. These enable speeds in excess of
150 knots to be achieved with a minimum mission endurance of 1.83 hours. The
engines are well separated to enhance the survivability of one should the other be
hit.

Survivability

Great emphasis has been placed on the ability of the Apache to absorb gun and
cannon fire and survive. For example, fuel tanks and main rotor spars have been
subjected to cannon fire, then continued to function for over 5 hours without
failing. The main gearbox has operated successfully without oil for over an hour
and the crew protective blast shields have been shown to be particularly effective.
The Black Hole IR suppression system markedly reduces the engine exhaust
temperatures and gives good protection against heat-seeking missiles. It is also a
very agile helicopter which in itself is a distinct asset in the fight to survive. The
Hellfire missiles are as close to a fire-and-forget system as has yet been devised,

since their guidance to the target can be left to a ground observer, also a great aid to survival. The similarities between these two helicopters are obvious and they represent the most formidable attack helicopters in the world. The Agusta A129 Mangusta represents Italy's first dedicated attack helicopter which is due in service in 1986 and which is similar in concept to the Hind and Apache, although very much smaller than both of them. Since the best weapon to counter a helicopter may be another helicopter, the chance of friendly and enemy helicopters meeting in aerial combat is high. The accurate and lethal cannon carried by attack helicopters, the Apache's Chain Gun, slaved to the IHADSS being particularly effective, give them a good air-to-air capability. A further enhancement would be to fit air-to-air missiles, and this approach is now being actively pursued by a number of nations, particularly for their utility helicopters which carry less armour or in-built ballistic protection.

Summary

Over the years the helicopter has evolved from an *ad hoc* weapons platform to a fully integrated weapon system capable of operating by day and night, in all but the worst weather. Its ability to deploy faster than any other battlefield system to combat unexpected incursions by armour is a characteristic which, in conjunction with its increasingly effective weapons, can make a substantial contribution to the land battle. Although attack helicopters have yet to prove themselves in an all-out war, they have operated successfully in Vietnam and Afghanistan. Now that second-generation attack helicopters are beginning to enter service, fitted with improved weapons, advanced sensor packages and better chances of surviving, they are likely to pose a severe threat to armoured formations. This fact is being widely recognised in many Western armies, many of which are now actively pursuing a requirement for dedicated attack helicopters, despite their high cost. The ability of these machines to fight alongside ground formations and to pose a threat to enemy rear areas is already causing consternation. Imaginative use of this new and increasingly effective weapons system could well give commanders the sort of battle-winning element provided first by the cavalry, then by tanks, using the two factors which they can produce most easily — surprise and shock effect.

SELF TEST QUESTIONS

QUESTION 1   What limitations make MG less than ideal as helicopter weapons?

Answer ....

....

....

QUESTION 2   What are the advantages of helicopter borne ATGW?

Answer a.   ....

b.   ....

c.   ....

d.   ....

QUESTION 3   What is IHADSS and how does it work?

Answer ....

....

....

QUESTION 4   Why have some nations been forced to accept armed helicopters?

Answer ....

....

....

QUESTION 5   What is a significant operational advantage of using large engines which operate at low power settings, such as in Hind?

Answer ....

....

....

QUESTION 6   What weapons can be carried by Apache?

Answer ....

....

....

QUESTION 7   What is the common type of sensor in TADS/PNVS used by both the pilot and the gunner?

Answer ....

....

....

QUESTION 8   What is the main disadvantage of the armed helicopter?

Answer ....

....

....

QUESTION 9   What is the main advantage enjoyed by armed and attack helicopters?

Answer ....

....

....

QUESTION 10 What exchange rates in terms of tanks lost per helicopter downed is being suggested as realistic?

Answer ....

....

....

Answers on page 136

7.
Survivability

The Problem

The equipment designers of today face the same problem of balancing the triangle of armaments, mobility and protection that mediaeval knights once faced. With only shield, chain mail tunic and helmet they were vulnerable to the lance, double-edged sword and mace, but being light and agile they stood a fair chance of avoiding the blows. Armour was later seen as a good way of reducing that vulnerability, but hand-in-hand with that protection came a loss of manoeuvrability and a greater likelihood of being hit. This is a similar problem to that met in the design of armoured vehicles and dealt with in some detail in Volume I of this series.

Until recently power and other limitations in light battlefield helicopters dictated that available payload should be used for fuel and role equipment with the minimum of armour protection. Survivability could be achieved by relying on the speed and agility of the aircraft, backed up by the use of good tactics and fieldcraft: in the helicopter this means the use of terrain in very low-level flight. But as combat helicopters have become more effective, so have countermeasures against them grown in scope, quality and quantity. Helicopters are prey to enemy armed helicopters, air defence guns and missile systems, vehicle-mounted armaments, small arms, massed artillery and multiple rocket fire. Fixed-wing aircraft, particularly slow-flying, also pose a threat.

Clearly something must be done to redress the balance, to allow the helicopter to continue fighting or, if this is not possible, to permit its return to base for repairs. Put another way, the helicopter designer is given the task, in order of priority, of saving the man, the machine and the mission.

It is not difficult to appreciate then that survivability depends on the product of a number of probabilities. In simple terms, what is required is a combat helicopter that is difficult to detect, difficult to hit when it has been detected, capable of continuing the mission even when it has been hit, and crashworthy if it is shot down. To achieve this complete package would be very expensive, and some compromises must be made as regards helicopter design and survivability equipment carried.

With a full suite of warning devices, countermeasures including weapons, and protective measures including armour, the helicopter would have to be large and heavy; it would therefore need more powerful engines and transmission systems. The cost would go up further and one element of the eternal triangle, mobility/manoeuvrability, would be likely to suffer.

Detection

Tactical Measures

Leaving aside the problems of indirect enemy fire where a helicopter can be hit unseen, a threat about which the crew can do little apart from anticipate where such fire might fall, a helicopter has to be seen to be hit. This involves a direct line of sight between the observer or sensor and the target. Minimising exposure to the enemy is, therefore, the first measure to be taken, and helicopter crews are accordingly trained to fly at very low level and make maximum use of the terrain to provide cover from view.

Positioning of Sights

Observation and weapon aiming sights also help to lower the chances of detection by allowing the helicopter to stand back from the enemy. Sights mounted under the nose of the Mi-24 Hind and in the nose of the AH-1S Cobra and AH-64 Apache require the helicopter to expose most of itself to observe or fire, but those in the cockpit roof (Bo-105, Gazelle and Lynx), or better still above the rotor mast, obviously reduce exposure and make the enemy's task more difficult. A good example of a roof-mounted sight is shown in Fig. 7.1. Similarly, helicopters with true fire and forget weapons will not have to unmask for long to aim and fire, unlike those with missiles which have to be guided onto the target and which are therefore at risk throughout the time of flight of the missile.

A helicopter has five distinctive signatures by which its presence can be detected: they are visual, acoustic, radar, infrared and electronic. All must be suppressed in one way or another.

Reduction of Visual Signature

Visual detection is achieved by the unaided eye, optical instruments such as binoculars and image intensifiers, or TV. How successful these are depend on the size and shape of the helicopter, its contrast with its background and movement. Obviously the smaller the machine the better. Ideally this should be enhanced by a paint scheme that reduces the contrast and apparently produces a false shape. Movement across country tends to attract attention, but even when in the hover, the sun glinting on the canopy or the rotor may give away a helicopter's position. The AH-1S and AH-64 use a flat plate canopy to reduce glint, shown in Fig. 7.2, and the appropriate paint to attenuate rotor flicker. The condition of the ground's surface is an important factor when in the hover, as sand, dust, snow or leaves recirculated through the main rotor can betray the presence of a helicopter. An astute observer can interpret isolated wildly swinging branches even if he cannot see the aircraft.

Acoustic Signature

It is often claimed that the acoustic signature of a combat helicopter is relatively unimportant, since the battlefield is not known for its solitude. Nevertheless, there are occasions, such as during the covert infiltration or recovery of patrols and in certain counter-insurgency operations when stealth is essential. Some of the noise can be attenuated by terrain features, but the presence of a helicopter will be obvious and a trained observer will have a good chance of pointing his weapon in the right direction before the helicopter becomes visible. The biggest contributors to noise are the main and tail rotors and engines. Many Soviet helicopters have rotors which turn at slow speed and therefore have low noise signatures. Blade tip shapes also help in this respect: both the AH-64 and UH-60 Black Hawk have aft swept tips, as shown in Fig. 7.3.

Fig. 7.1 Avimo-Ferranti AF-532 roof mounted sight on a Gazelle

Fig. 7.2 Huey Cobra's flat plate canopy

MH–H

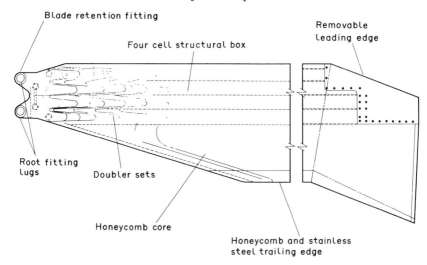

Fig. 7.3 Apache main rotor blade showing swept tip

The ideal is to have a helicopter without a tail rotor such as the Sikorksy XH-59A (advancing blade concept) and Kamov's helicopters which all use co-axial, contra-rotating rotor systems, and the Hughes No Tail Rotor (NOTAR) helicopter. The scissor tail rotor on the AH-64 has offset blades which cut through clean air; it is therefore more efficient: its speed, and thus noise, are comparatively low.

Radar Signature

A target illuminated by radar produces a signature known as radar reflectivity or radar cross-section. The amount of energy reflected is a function of target size, shape, angle relative to the beam, material electrical properties and the characteristics of the radar itself. Detection thus depends upon the radar and its processing of information, the target's signature and the ability of the operator to interpret what he can see on his screen. A radar's detection range and its ability to find helicopters in ground clutter can be degraded by reductions in the helicopter's radar cross-section. Control of the shape of the helicopter and use of the correct materials in its structure are two basic methods of achieving this. Taking into account where possible the most probable angles from which the helicopter will be seen on radar, shapes can be chosen, subject to other design constraints, which can reflect the energy anywhere but back to the radar.

Even in the hover the helicopter has many moving parts, such as rotors, which are susceptible to radar detection. But the use of conductive coatings and broadband radar absorbing material can lower the risk.

IR Signature

Any object with a temperature above absolute zero radiates IR energy. Because of atmospheric absorption this energy appears in the 1–3, 3–5 and 8–13 micrometre wavelengths. The hot metal in a helicopter engine emits in the lowest band, while the exhaust gases are in the middle band. The first generation of IR suppressors consisted of scoops over the exhaust to deflect it upwards into the rotor downwash and to shield the hot metal from the direct view of an IR-seeking missile. More modern suppressors use large quantities of ambient air to cool the hot metal and to dilute the exhaust gas to lower the plume signature. This is known as the Black Hole concept and is similar to that shown in Fig. 7.4.

Fig. 7.4 Lynx prototype IR suppression system

Combined with IR low reflective paint used to resist detection by thermal imaging systems in the 8–13 micrometre band, the effect is to reduce the range of heat-seeking missiles and to make feasible the use of IR jammers and decoy flares. Soviet helicopters usually have engines which run at comparatively low turbine entry temperatures and thus low exhaust temperatures. Cooling air is drawn into the gearbox, often through an intake above the engines, and helps to cool hot metal and the exhaust plume.

Miscellaneous Electromagnetic Emitters

There are many items of equipment on board a helicopter which by their use will give its position away. Direction finders can pinpoint radio emissions, and Doppler navigators, radar altimeters, laser range finders/designators, and indeed any other active systems are all liable to detection. They must therefore be used as infrequently as possible, voice communications kept to the minimum and the helicopter kept on the move, behind cover.

Survival on the Ground

Before leaving the matter of detection it is as well to remember that combat helicopters spend more time on the ground than they do in the air. Concealment and camouflage are therefore essential and not only from the view of an enemy reconnaissance pilot but from the sensors on board his aircraft. Skid-equipped helicopters are difficult to move, those with wheels a little less so, and all types are cumbersome to camouflage. No satisfactory solutions have been found, yet they are urgently needed.

Engagement

The Tactical Problem

If, despite all efforts, a helicopter is detected it can escape being hit. Minimising exposure may not give the enemy time to aim their weapons and good tactics will provide some protection: for example, moving to a new position immediately after attacking a target from ambush. By opening fire at maximum range the enemy's chance of achieving a hit are reduced. Because well-sited weapons are mutually supporting, however, staying out of range of one enemy weapon may bring the helicopter within range of another.

Agility

An agile helicopter, and therefore one which is elusive to the enemy, is to be desired. While speed is important in certain circumstances, agility from and to the hover is more highly prized among NATO nations. This simply means acceleration and deceleration in all dimensions. A power margin that permits a rapid rate of climb when above cover and an ability to descend and establish a new hover quickly without striking the ground is required. In addition, a helicopter must be able to accelerate sideways to avoid bursts of fire. The Hind can sustain 3G turns and any future helicopter should be able to match this at least and also accept negative G for a few seconds.

Warning Sensors

To see without being seen is the ideal state; the reverse can be disastrous, but something may be done about this fact if a helicopter crew can be made aware of it. Warning the crew of the presence of enemy weapon systems therefore plays a large part in the avoidance of being hit. A radar warning receiver which can provide an immediate indication of a radar, which is associated with a weapon that threatens the helicopter, will alert the crew to the danger and help it decide what to do. A receiver that can detect fire control, missile guidance and associated tracking radars and which associated weapon system poses the greatest threat is necessary. Interpretation of the display was a problem with the early receivers, there being no doubt that a crew desires to be able to form an accurate mental picture of the situation from a single glance. Using the same processor and display as the radar warning receiver will in due course be a laser warner, which will be able to detect and identify range-finders and designators and laser beam-riding missiles.

The need for a sensing device to dispense IR decoy flares led to the development of an IR missile detection system. One such is actually a short-range pulse doppler radar which establishes a continuous radar ring around the helicopter. Any missile exhibiting the proper closing velocity characteristics triggers the decoy flares automatically. Such a system only gives warning of imminent missile impact; is warning perhaps of a missile launch required?

What is more difficult to warn against are those threat systems which are not radiating: any concealed operator who is using merely his eyes, binoculars or other optical aids has a distinct advantage and every helicopter crew must guard against blundering into areas where visually sited weapons can be brought to bear. Work is proceeding on the development of optical warning devices.

Giving warning of small arms and machine gun fire can be achieved by acoustic means. This relies on the detection of the shock wave and therefore the bullet must still be travelling supersonically. Depending upon the calibre of the weapon, ranges will be comparatively short. An approximate direction of fire can be indicated and, clearly, evasive action can only be taken against the second and subsequent bursts of fire.

Wires can bring down a helicopter in peace and war. Thorough flight planning and careful and continuous lookout are essential. Electronic means of detecting wires have been under study for a number of years and millimetric wave radars and lasers seem to be the most promising; the detection of live HT cables by sensing their associated magnetic fields has already been proved to be practicable. Stabilisation in relation to the helicopter's constantly changing attitude in flight and psychological factors, however, poses considerable problems. Simple wire cutters and deflectors may be the solution.

Countermeasures

Receiving timely warning of a threat is one thing, but the consequent reaction is what is important. Descending or turning away could be all that is needed, but active countermeasures may be more effective. The most positive is to open fire on the offending system, if appropriate; if not, radar or IR jammers and chaff or decoy flares could cause sufficient degradation to prevent the helicopter being hit.

Chaff consists of a mass of small dipole reflectors which constitute a larger return than the helicopter within the radar beam. Chaff, unlike a radar jammer, does not depend on the enemy radar frequency apart from the fact that the dipoles must be cut to some frequency equal to or lower than the radar frequency and dispensed in sufficient quantity. Launched as soon as a tracking radar locks onto the helicopter, the chaff has the effect of breaking the lock and forcing the radar operator to return to the search mode to re-establish lock. This takes a finite time during which the crew can take other evasive measures or open fire. Combined with a radar warning receiver, chaff can be dispensed automatically and in the correct direction. A cockpit control unit allows crew selection of the dispensing mode, the number of units to be fired, the interval between units and groups of units, and group intervals. A typical dispenser can carry 60 chaff units and the effect can be seen in Fig. 7.5 which shows a US UH-1 emitting a chaff cloud.

FIG. 7.5 Chaff dispensed by a UH-1

The same dispenser, tied in with the missile approach detector, can be programmed also to fire IR decoy flares automatically. Given imminent missile impact, manual ejection by the crew is useless. Television pictures of Israeli jets attacking targets in the Lebanon in 1982 showed them regularly dispensing flares to decoy any heat-seeking missiles that might be fired against them. They did not appear, however, to be linked with a missile approach detector. An IR decoy flare being dropped by a US Chinook is shown in Fig. 7.6.

FIG. 7.6 A Chinook helicopter drops an IR decoy flare

Such missiles can also be decoyed by an IR jammer. Electrically-fired and omnidirectional, it may consist of a cylindrical source which emits modulated IR energy several times greater than that of the helicopter itself. The aim is to generate false information as to the true location of the helicopter and thus confuse the IR seeker.

Radar jammers have been used since the Second World War, but until recently have been too large, heavy and complex for employment in helicopters. But the ALQ-136 in the AH-1S, for example, weighs less than 20 kg and occupies very little space. Because it may only take a few seconds to detect a target and acquire the necessary tracking data, a jammer has to deny this information for periods greater than about 3 or 4 seconds. The ALQ-136 is passive until illuminated by an enemy radar which has locked on to the helicopter. It automatically analyses the incoming signals and determines from their characteristics whether they emanate from an enemy radar. If so, electronic countermeasures are applied to defeat the range and angle measurement circuits in the radar. The ALQ-136 can jam two enemy radars simultaneously.

Finally, a helicopter may be able to use a variety of smokes in self-defence. A green or brown smoke to blend in with the background could provide ordinary screening from enemy view, while other types of smoke could degrade laser beams and IR seekers.

Tolerance to Fire

When designing a helicopter which is to tolerate fire it is vital to be clear about the calibre against which protection is required and its purpose. If close to a nuclear burst there is probably little that can be done, depending on range, besides providing some protection against blast, heat and flying debris. If a missile strikes, then luck will generally dictate whether the crew can do anything to save the helicopter or themselves. But against 7.62 mm, 12.7 mm, 14.5 mm and even isolated 23 mm API and HEI strikes protection can be provided. However, machine gun fire is usually in bursts and to achieve protection against multiple hits of even 12.7 mm is far from simple or cheap.

In decreasing order of effectiveness an enemy desires to destroy the helicopter and kill the crew, or force it to land immediately, or prevent it from continuing with its mission.

The user, and therefore the helicopter designer, is keen to deny any degree of satisfaction to the enemy. But his first priority is to save the crew; to save the mission the appropriate role equipment must remain operational. Inevitably trade-offs will arise in the degree of protection against cost, complexity, space and weight. Designers endeavour to keep the most vulnerable areas as compact as possible and to spread out duplicated components and systems to minimise the chances of total failure. But this could mean a larger helicopter and increase the risk of detection.

Tolerance to fire is best considered at the design stage when ballistic tolerance, redundancy and separation, armour and fire suppression can be assessed. Careful selection of the materials used and their thickness can now achieve ballistic immunity from certain calibres for many parts of a helicopter: for example, rotor heads and blades, drive shafts, structures and flight controls. One of the advantages of composite materials is good ballistic tolerance to HE rounds. A Kevlar fibreglass shield with high blast and 23 mm fragment resistance separates the pilot from the co-pilot/gunner in the AH-64 to minimise the chances of both crew members being incapacitated by the same burst of fire from the front. Both cockpits have spall-resistant windshields. The HIND is similarly well-protected.

Another form of tolerance is to build transmissions which can continue to operate for at least 30 minutes or more after the oil has been lost. Both the UH-60 and AH-64 have this facility.

Redundancy is attractive for reasons of safety in peacetime, apart from the benefits in war. Duplicated, or even triplicated, systems which are widely separated confer a large measure of survivability. Engines, electrical, hydraulic and fuel systems and flight controls can all be, at least, duplicated.

Fly-by-wire systems, which use electrical impulses through a wire from the pilot's controls to operate control jacks are now being introduced. Such systems are very lightweight, allowing duplication for a minimal increase in weight. The wires can be widely separated throughout the airframe, adding to the aircraft's survivability.

To prevent a helicopter's weight increasing steeply, very selective use of armour, incorporated at the design/development stage, must be made. In the Mi-24 the Russians seek to provide protection at least up to 12.7 mm calibre for the crew and critical aircraft components; NATO helicopters rely less heavily on armour. Colocated engines may have an armoured separation plate and crews have armoured floors, seats and body armour as shown in Fig. 7.7. But it is extremely hard to find a material that is resistant to penetration by the larger machine gun calibres and high velocity projectiles and fragments and that is, at the same time, light and cheap. Kevlar laminates and aluminium oxide ceramics have been used successfully. Body armour obviously must not be bulky, and a major problem yet to be solved is that of protecting the crew's heads.

Fuel fires or explosions are likely to be catastrophic. Fuel tanks and lines can incorporate a material which automatically seals holes, and they can be surrounded by void-filling foam which reduces the onset of conditions which could trigger an explosion. A fire detection system combined with small extinguishers around the tanks reduces the chances of a fire taking hold or a fuel explosion.

Crashworthiness

A great deal of effort in recent years has been devoted to the problems of saving the crew and limiting damage to the aircraft to the extent that it can be repaired in the event of a crash. New US military helicopters must now comply with certain crashworthy design criteria. Other countries are beginning to follow this example.

In general terms a designer has five crash-survivability objectives. They are, first to maintain a protective shell around the crew and passengers, second to make the interior of this shell injury-free, third to limit the G load on the occupants, fourth to prevent a post-crash fire and fifth to allow immediate escape.

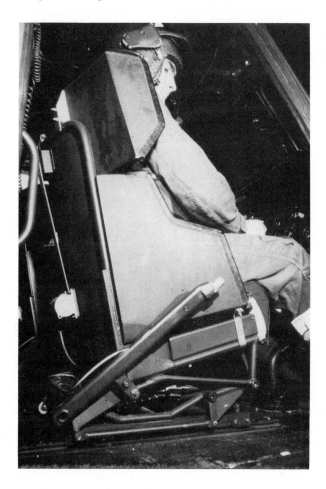

FIG. 7.7 A Puma armoured crew seat

To maintain a protective shell, mass items such as engines must withstand load factors of 20 G vertically and longitudinally and 18 G laterally. These loads equate roughly to impacts of 12.9 m/s (42 ft/s) in the first case and 9.2 m/s (30 ft/s) laterally, although G loads will peak at higher values momentarily. The airframe structure should provide roll-over protection and the energy-absorbing landing gear should be able to decelerate the helicopter at an average 9 or 10 G through a distance of perhaps half a metre or so. At a vertical speed of 10.7 m/s (35 ft/s) this will prevent the fuselage touching the ground.

All interior equipment must be restrained to high G loads. Occupants must be positioned so that they will be free from head strikes and from being trapped or cut on sharp edges.

Limiting the load on the occupants is achieved by crash-attenuating seats which may have a movement of about 0.3 m (12 in). Five-belt safety harnesses stop the risk of slipping free.

The only practical way to prevent a post-crash fire is to contain the fuel. This is achieved by having sufficiently strong tanks that are positioned well away from ignition sources and anything that might penetrate them in a crash. Fuel and vent lines must also be crash-resistant with self-sealing breakaway valves. Fuel spillage can be minimised by installing suction fuel pumps.

Safety harnesses with a single point buckle allow rapid release and emergency escape through jettisonable doors or windows. Ejection seats are feasible, but the problems associated with jettisoning the rotors first or ejecting sideways have so far proved to be insuperable. Thus the thrust of survival technology has been towards surviving a crash.

Summary

Survivability in a combat helicopter is a function of many interrelated factors which include the threat, tactics, training, aircraft performance, target acquisition and engagement, command and control, and survivability equipment. Survivability for its own sake is valueless; the helicopter and crew must survive in order to carry out their battlefield tasks so that they can contribute to the all-arms battle.

Survivability for attack helicopters can be measured by such exchange ratios as the number of targets destroyed per helicopter loss, and for reconnaissance helicopters by the length of time on task per helicopter loss.

Inevitably survivability equipment adds to the weight and cost of a helicopter and consumes space and electrical power. These penalties must be assessed against the degree of protection provided to reach an optimum package and this package must then be balanced against any deleterious effects that it may have on aircraft performance and weapons and fuel load. There could come a point when the helicopter is so well protected that it loses effectiveness in its primary roles.

It is then for the military and financial staffs to decide whether it is better to go to war with a cheap and cheerful helicopter relying on stealth and agility to survive or a heavy, well-protected and expensive machine that can trade blow for blow with the enemy. National resources will dictate the answer and, for all but the Super-Powers, this probably lies somewhere between the two extremes.

SELF TEST QUESTIONS

QUESTION 1   What are the four main objectives for a designer to achieve when considering helicopter survivability?

Answer ....

....

QUESTION 2   What are a helicopter's five distinctive signatures, any one of which can betray its presence?

Answer ....

....

QUESTION 3   List design factors associated with normal detection.

Answer ....

....

QUESTION 4   In what respects should a combat helicopter be agile?

Answer ....

....

QUESTION 5   Give four types of warning device that helicopters may soon carry.

Answer ....

....

QUESTION 6   What is the purpose of an IR jammer?

Answer ....

....

QUESTION 7   How may enemy fire up to a given calibre be tolerated?

Answer ....

....

QUESTION 8   Why is armour only used sparingly?

Answer ....

....

QUESTION 9   List ways of preventing post-crash fires.

Answer ....

....

QUESTION 10   What factors must be assessed when considering the installation of any piece of survivability equipment?

Answer ....

....

Answers on page 137

8.
Advanced Features

The State of Technology

Since the end of the Second World War the military helicopter has benefited from the quickening technical revolution. The results are a vastly enhanced flight performance, formidable firepower, reduced vulnerability to enemy fire, advanced avionics and more simple maintenance; most important, the ever-upward spiral of production and operating costs has been slowed. The introduction of the turbine engine was an important advance in terms of power-to-weight ratio and reliability compared with its piston predecessor; in the 1940s rotor blades were composed of laminated wood and fabric, in the 1960s of steel and aluminium and in the 1980s of titanium and composite materials; transmissions and drive trains have progressed from 180 hp to 13,000 hp.

In terms of sophistication the helicopter is almost in a position to challenge fixed-wing aircraft, and this state of affairs has been achieved in just 40 years compared to the 80 years since the Wright brothers first flew. The helicopter now stands on the threshold of another period of dynamic technical growth which will embrace much wider use of composite materials, fuel efficient engines, advanced systems to reduce crew workload and permit operations at night and in adverse weather, and optical flight controls; continuing efforts will be made to reduce the bugbear of all helicopters, vibration. It is probably true to say that there is no part of a helicopter that is not the subject of development work somewhere. In this chapter we will look at some examples of advanced features and systems that may be retrofitted into existing helicopters or be designed into the next generation.

Materials

The materials with which helicopter airframes, engines and other components have been built have played a key role in the evolution of the helicopter. The initial use of composite materials was limited to the manufacture of secondary structural parts made of glass fibre impregnated with epoxy resin. But when the new fibres, particularly carbon and Kevlar which were lighter but had better stiffness characteristics than glass composites, arrived the advantages were quickly appreciated. They have reduced weight, longer fatigue life, less maintenance, greater tolerance to ballistic damage and they can be moulded into complex, highly efficient aerodynamic shapes not possible with conventional metals. All these attributes lead to lower costs. Rotor blades were the first major component to use this new technology, not then with the primary intention of reducing weight, but to increase fatigue life. Now the use of composites has spread to rotor hubs, landing gear and fuselage components; soon will come bearingless rotors and aeroelastically tailored rotor blades.

Perhaps the most exciting project is the US Army's Advanced Composite Airframe Programme (ACAP) which calls for an all-composite, non-metallic fuselage using an existing drive train. The major aims are to make a weight saving of 22% compared to an equivalent metal aircraft and achieve a 17% reduction in cost, while at the same time meeting the established requirements for crashworthiness, ballistic tolerance, reduced radar cross-section, and reliability and maintainability. High-strength carbon fibre-reinforced plastic, glass fibre and impact-resistant Kevlar will all be used.

Bell Helicopters and Sikorsky are building three airframes each, with the first flight scheduled for March 1984 and a flight evaluation programme lasting until January 1985. The aim of the programme is to develop a composites technology base which can be applied to the next generation of lightweight US Army helicopters.

The European airframe manufacturers are not very far behind. Indeed it was in Europe that the first composite rotor blades were developed and introduced on an experimental basis. In 1966 Aérospatiale and Messerschmitt-Bölkow-Blohm (MBB) signed an agreement to develop jointly such a blade, and two years later it appeared, consisting of glass fibre impregnated with epoxy resin and surrounding a monobloc core of honeycomb material. Both these companies have continued to push ahead, as have Westland Helicopters and Agusta with its A-129 attack helicopter which has an airframe skin composed of 70% composites. A typical composite main rotor blade is shown in Fig. 8.1.

British Experimental Rotor Programme (BERP)

The Westland Lynx III mock-up, exhibited at the Farnborough Air Display in September 1982, sported an unusual rotor system. Quite obvious were the unique paddle-shaped blade tips which, by reducing compressibility and drag in the advancing blade and delaying the stall in the retreating blade, will allow the helicopter cruising speeds up to 200 knots. One such blade tip is shown in Fig. 8.2. To achieve this speed, however, will necessitate in addition certain airframe drag reductions. The rotor blades are a composite of glass and carbon fibre-reinforced plastic with the aerofoil section changing along the span. They are expected to fly for the first time in 1985 and offer the following impressive list of advantages:

1. A 25% increase in payload or a decreased rotor size (blade chord or diameter) for the same payload.
2. Higher forward speeds.
3. Reduced power required and therefore more power available and lower fuel consumption.
4. Better manoeuvrability and agility.
5. Improved hover characteristics.

6. Easier to manufacture.
7. Ability to retrofit to existing aircraft.
8. Increased fatigue life.
9. Reduced noise.
10. Increased ballistic tolerance.
11. Reduced radar cross-section.
12. Lower life cycle costs.

FIG. 8.1 Composite main rotor blade

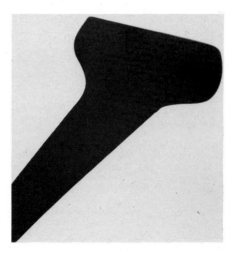

FIG. 8.2 British experimental rotor blade

Engines

No change in the next decade is expected to change the use of turboshaft engines in helicopters. Progress is therefore likely to be directed towards improving fuel consumption, reducing weight, increasing reliability and easing maintenance in the field, and lowering development and production costs. Instead of the hydraulic-mechanical metering of fuel, it will soon be standard practice to have such an important function carried out electronically by what is known as a full authority digital engine control (FADEC). Electronic control is much more sensitive and accurate and permits the engines to be run much more closely to their operating limits. The matching of torque between twin engines is automatic, as is hands-off starting. FADEC also has the ability to monitor the condition of various parts of the engine, thus enabling more accurate assessments to be made of wear and tear, with a consequent reduction in overhaul costs.

A FADEC can be mounted on the engine or the airframe and for an engine the size of the Rolls-Royce Gem weighs about 6 kg. In due course engine designers will have to take into account the probability of using synthetic fuels which may require different starting techniques and which may also possess unaccustomed impurities.

Flight Controls

Mechanical flight controls are comparatively heavy and complex, and require regular maintenance. Fly-by-wire or fly-by-light (fibre optic) technology almost eliminates these disadvantages by replacing the mechanical control rods by electronic links between the pilot's controls and the rotor actuators. Furthermore, this active control technology (ACT) offers many positive advantages. Quicker response to the pilot's control movements permits the helicopter's attitude to be changed more rapidly and the full capability of the rotor system can be used to expand the flight envelope and improve manoeuvrability. The pilot's workload can be reduced, because ACT leads to a more stable helicopter by decoupling rolling, pitching and yawing motions; hovering and hover turns will be simpler, and this will ease the problems associated with weapon aiming. Another major advantage will be dramatically improved survivability, not only through better manoeuvrability but also because vulnerability to fire will be so much reduced: the very thin wires or fibre-optics will be less likely to be hit than control rods, and they can easily be duplicated. Perhaps most important of all will be reduced weight, costs and maintenance, and higher integrity. There is a drawback to fly-by-wire, however, and that is its susceptibility to electromagnetic interference and pulses. For this reason, although development will continue, it may be by-passed in favour of fly-by-light as the primary system; fly-by-wire could be used as a back-up as in the AH-64 Apache and A-129 Mangusta.

An American fly-by-light programme is known as the advanced digital/optical control system (ADOCS).

Vibration is one of the helicopter designer's greatest problems. New control technology should offer a much smoother ride with much less vibration and susceptibility to turbulence, and by using higher harmonic control (HHC) vibration can be further suppressed to provide a level of stability that would allow the precision delivery of all on-board weapons, and reduce crew and metal fatigue. HHC is an electronic computer-controlled vibration suppression system which senses and cancels vibrations in the airframe by high-frequency feathering of the rotor blades. Accelerometers sense the vibration and pass signals to an electronic control unit which converts them for analysis by the microprocessor. The correct amount of blade feathering is the result, and the necessary signals flash back to the actuators which are inserted in place of the ordinary fixed links between the mixer unit and the stationary swashplate.

Aids to Control

Crew Workload

Due to the effectiveness of ground-based weapons and sensors today's battlefield helicopters are forced to operate at very low levels amongst a variety of obstacles. The demands on the crew are high and become even greater when darkness falls or the weather deteriorates. The purpose of reducing the cockpit workload is to give the crew more time to pay attention to what is happening on the battlefield so that they can make a bigger contribution to the action, and to delay the onset of fatigue. Depending upon the success of the automatic devices now being contemplated and their cost, the return to a single-man cockpit may be made. Whether for one crewman or two, future cockpits are likely to be characterised by multi-mode displays, strip instruments and management systems. Options for display on a cathode ray tube (CRT) or flat panel might be flight information for cruising or hovering, power systems, weapons status, navigation data, communications information and a diagrammatic representation of the tactical situation; a cockpit might have two or three CRTs or flat panel displays which are expected to replace CRTs. The pilot will be relieved of many routine tasks, thus leaving him with more time to take decisions concerning the aircraft and the tactical situation. In addition, weight and space will be saved.

Another way of reducing crew workload may be to use direct voice input (DVI). Trials are already under way to see what effect voice control can have on workload. It can be used for certain housekeeping duties such as radio control and calling of displays. For example, the required scale, orientation and look forward capabilities on a moving map display could be controlled by voice command.

Cockpit Management System

To communicate in code on different radios and differing frequencies, to navigate at very low level in poor visibility and to keep up-to-date with the changing combat situation is very demanding on the crew. By using a computer-based mission management system all the key information concerning radios, codes, callsigns, frequencies and other information can be displayed in the cockpit; and the crew can dispense with a hefty wad of paper. A battlefield mission management system is shown in use in Fig. 8.3, installed in a British Army Lynx.

MH–I

FIG. 8.3 A battlefield mission management system

A further significant advantage for the crew and operations staff is that the time spent on pre-flight briefing can be drastically shortened. A portable solid state data store, little larger than a cigarette packet, can be plugged into a ground terminal to extract the necessary information and transfer it to the helicopter where it is simply slotted into the airborne installation. The ground terminal consists of a keyboard computer with a visual display unit. It is updated manually by an operations clerk or automatically by means of an automatic data processing system.

Full colour displays which can graphically represent the helicopter's flight path in the tactical arena are under development, and these will help the crew to avoid dangerous areas. A management system such as this can also be used to collect data for monitoring components as part of a maintenance programme.

Artificial intelligence computer systems may have an application in future helicopter cockpits. They will be able to assist in making decisions from a mass of confused information: giving warning of impending failure and the necessary action to be taken; choosing the order of targets to be attacked to make best use of on-board weapons and the terrain. Much research needs to be done in this field and its success will depend upon the funds available.

Payload Margin Indicator
Such is the nature of the battlefield that there is often neither the time nor the inclination to weigh the load to be carried, either men or material. A rule of

thumb is used for combat-equipped troops and no more than a guess for any inanimate object. There is an obvious danger, therefore, of under-utilisation or overloading.

A cockpit indicator which gives a continual readout of the payload still available would neatly solve the problem. Using a microprocessor, already fed with the relevant aircraft data, a system would compute the margin and associated centre of gravity positions, helicopter altitude, temperature and the extent of uneven ground would all be taken into account. The weight of underslung loads could also be measured.

Indications would be by means of audio and visual signals. The Royal Aircraft Establishment at Farnborough has designed an indicator which uses light-emitting diodes to show the movement of the centre of gravity and when the limits are exceeded. An audio signal warns when no more payload can be carried.

Obstacle Warning

The greatest threat to battlefield helicopters, unconnected with the enemy, are wires and in particular power cables. As helicopters are forced to fly lower and lower in ever worse weather the need for some kind of warning of "live" and "dead" wires becomes more urgent.

Various laser and electromagnetic systems have so far been tested and further developments continue. In general terms the system scans all round the helicopter to pick up wires coming in diagonally to intercept the flight path as well as those strung across it. Detection ranges of over 1000 metres can be achieved.

Although not a warning system, wire cutters could be mounted above the cockpit and deflectors below to cater for those wires not seen. A cutter may not be able to cope with the heaviest wires.

Sighting Systems

Mast-mounted Sights

The first generation of sights mounted above the rotor mast will soon be in service on operational helicopters. They will be stabilised to compensate for the helicopter's movement and the vibration of the rotor blades and their very position eliminates centre of gravity problems, a drawback of nose-mounted sights.

Those helicopters which presently mount observation or weapon-aiming sights have them located in the roof (e.g. Lynx, Gazelle and Bo-105), in the nose (e.g. AH-1S Cobra and AH-64) or even under it (Mi-24 Hind D and E). The lower the position of the sight, the more the helicopter must expose itself for the gunner to see over cover. Modern battlefield radars are well able to detect the main or tail rotors of a helicopter, although it may be screened optically by foliage. Sun flashing on the rotor blades or the canopy may also reveal the presence of a helicopter.

But if mounted between 2 and 3 feet above the mast, the sight enables the crew to view the enemy with the rest of the helicopter behind cover. It should be appreciated, however, that a very accurate hover indeed will need to be established, and this may even be beyond the capability of an automatic hover control. With only the sight exposed, detection and engagement of the helicopter is very difficult. Survivability is enhanced significantly in this way and should result in improved exchange ratios of targets destroyed to helicopter losses.

Mast-mounted sights can be used for a variety of purposes, the more important being observation, target acquisition, designation and engagement, and early warning. Because missiles must be mounted comparatively low on a helicopter the advantages of having a mast-mounted sight are largely destroyed if the helicopter has to unmask to fire. Fortunately, however, it is not difficult to arrange for the missile's launch electronics to provide for the missile itself to fly up to the line of sight to the target and therefore clear any obstacle to the front, provided the helicopter hovers sufficiently far back from that obstacle. An armed helicopter with a mast-mounted sight is shown in Fig. 8.4.

There are different methods of transmitting information and commands to and from the sight, but it is usual to make use of a hollow mast. The temptation to cram all sorts of devices into the sight is overwhelming, but has to be resisted for weight, size and stabilisation reasons. A typical installation might weight about 70 kg. It would include one or more of the following items of equipment: TV camera, low light level TV camera, laser rangefinder/designator and thermal imager. Naturally, the necessary gyros, boresight mechanism and cooling for any thermal imager accompany these items.

Fig. 8.4 A mast-mounted sight on a Hughes Defender

The pictures from the cameras are displayed in the cockpit on a CRT and as may be expected their quality is not as good as with direct view optics when the gunner is able to look directly through his telescope mounted in a nose or roof sight.

Thermal Imaging

As the demands to be able to fly and fight at night and in poor visibility have become more insistent, so strenuous efforts have been made to develop thermal imagers for incorporation into gunners' sights and in the case of the Apache to give the pilot his own thermal imager so that he can see as well as his gunner. This is an expensive solution that takes up weight and space, and for most current combat helicopters the pilot has to make do with image intensification night vision goggles which at least allow safe flight in conditions of starlight only.

For the gunner the thermal radiation from a target is acquired by means of a scanning system and infrared detectors which look at the scene. The result is reconstituted as a visual picture, usually on a monochrome TV in the cockpit. Better, however, is to project the picture through an eyepiece via a CRT inserted into the downtube of the normal daylight sight.

Thermal imaging exploits the link between the peak infrared emission of objects and the atmospheric attenuation windows in the electromagnetic spectrum of 3–5 micrometres and 8–14 micrometres. As a result a thermal imager, which in aircraft is sometimes called a forward looking infrared (FLIR), can detect the temperature differences between objects such as a tank and natural vegetation to produce a heat picture.

Because helicopter crews are keen to be able to detect and identify targets at night as far away as possible, appropriate thermal imagers are comparatively large, heavy and expensive. Space, however, is usually at a premium, but the smaller the optics the less the range. Nevertheless, thermal imagers will allow tank targets to be detected at ranges over 2 km in pitch darkness; furthermore, they substantially improve the observer's ability to see though battlefield smoke and haze by day.

Summary

In the next few years military helicopter operators can be expected to take a close look at the wide array of advanced features that will be on offer. Careful assessments will be made of cost, weight, volume and power consumption against the increase in effectiveness. Many features will no doubt become obsolete before they can even enter production. But it is certain that advanced technology will greatly enhance the helicopter and its capabilities.

                    SELF TEST QUESTIONS

QUESTION 1   List some of the advantages of using composite materials.

             Answer ....

             ....

QUESTION 2   What improvements in turbine engines are expected during the
             next decade?

             Answer ....

             ....

QUESTION 3   What advantages does a FADEC offer?

             Answer ....

             ....

QUESTION 4   What forms of flight controls might replace the present
             mechanical controls?

             Answer ....

             ....

QUESTION 5   List three ways of reducing the hazard of wire strikes.

             Answer ....

             ....

QUESTION 6   What are the advantages offered by sights mounted above the
             rotor mast?

             Answer ....

             ....

QUESTION 7 What equipment might be found in a mast mounted sight?

Answer ....

....

QUESTION 8 In what part of the EM spectrum do thermal imagers operate?

Answer ....

....

QUESTION 9 Down to what light conditions can the most modern night vision goggles operate?

Answer ....

....

Answers on page 138

9.

Future Trends

Introduction

There are several ideas which are currently under development or investigation which could significantly enhance the performance of battlefield helicopters. In reviewing some of these, the term helicopter may seem to be a misnomer, in the sense that the rotor, or rotors, is not the sole means of obtaining lift and thrust for all of the vehicles considered. Nevertheless, the application of some of these ideas, if successful, will produce a vehicle which would be directly competitive with the pure helicopter.

Helicopter Speed Limitations

One significant drawback of the helicopter is its limited performance in forward flight, both in absolute speed and in manoeuvrability. Whilst for 'nap of the earth' operations the forward speed limitation may not be critical, because of the difficulties of high-speed flight very close to the ground, limitations on manoeuvrability impose their own constraints. In order to understand the developments which are needed to improve the situation, it is necessary to appreciate the cause of these limitations.

Manoeuvrability can be defined as the rapidity with which a vehicle can change speed or direction. In order to do either of these, it is necessary to provide a force acting in the direction in which acceleration is required. The magnitude of the force needed to produce a given acceleration, and hence a given change in speed or direction, depends on the weight of the vehicle being accelerated. A useful way of comparing the manoeuvrability of vehicles of differing weights is therefore given by dividing the manoeuvring force available by the weight of the vehicle. This ratio is referred to as the load factor. Since by far the largest force available for manoeuvring a helicopter is the thrust of the main rotor, the ratio of maximum main rotor thrust to the all-up weight is a good measure of the inherent manoeuvrability of the helicopter.

Both the forward speed and manoeuvrability limitations have the same root cause. To understand this consider Fig. 9.1. This is a plan view of a helicopter rotor viewed from above. The solid line indicates the local speed of the blades in the hover. This varies from zero at the rotor hub to a maximum at the blade tips and is the same for all azimuth positions of the blade. When the helicopter moves forwards, however, the speed of the advancing blade, on the right-hand side of the rotor disc shown, is increased, whilst the speed of the retreating blade, on the left-hand side of the disc, is reduced. This is shown by the dotted line. The lift available from any section of the blade is proportional to the square of the speed, and for a single rotor helicopter the lift on the two sides of the disc must be equal, otherwise the helicopter would roll over and a crash could result. So the loss of lifting capability on the retreating side of the disc cannot be compensated by the increase in lift available on the advancing side. The maximum lift potentially available from a single helicopter rotor therefore reduces as the forward speed of the helicopter increases.

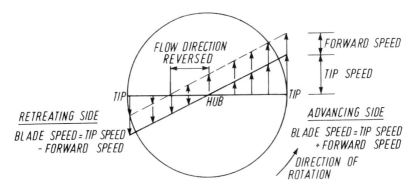

Fig. 9.1 Speed differential across a rotor

In fact, this situation becomes so bad at high forward speeds that the retreating blade, which is moving most slowly, will tend to stall. One possible way of preventing this would be to speed up the whole rotor. The problem is not solved by this, however, because another problem appears on the other side of the rotor disc. At the tip of the advancing blade, its speed relative to the air, which is the sum of the helicopter forward speed and the rotor tip speed, approaches the speed of sound. This causes, among other things, a very large drag increase and a loss of lift. The net result of all this is that there is an almost fixed optimum tip speed for all helicopters and also a severe forward speed limitation. This is illustrated in Fig. 9.2.

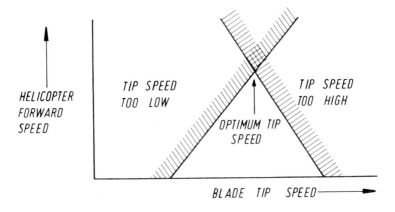

Fig. 9.2 Optimum tip speed and forward speed limitations

In fact, the maximum lift potentially available at low forward speeds cannot normally be utilised because of power limitations. The load factor achievable by a conventional helicopter then tends to increase rather slowly with increased helicopter forward speed until the speed limitations referred to above are encountered. The overall effect on the forward flight manoeuvre capability of a conventional helicopter is indicated in Fig. 9.3.

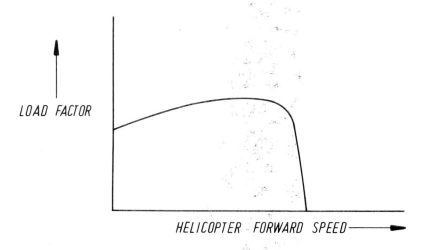

FIG. 9.3 Effect of load factor on forward speed

Aerodynamic Developments

One way of alleviating the problem described above is to equip the helicopter with small fixed wings. These develop lift which is proportional to the forward speed of the helicopter squared and can therefore compensate, to some extent, for the loss of rotor lift. It is not feasible to provide too much lift from a fixed wing, however, as the rotor blades need to maintain some lift to prevent them from flapping down and striking the helicopter body. The weight of the wing will reduce the payload of the helicopter and it will have its own drag. Another disadvantage is that the area of the wing reduces the available rotor lift in the hover. If rolling take-offs are used, which are popular with the Soviets, for example, this is not serious. The wing compensates for some of these disadvantages by providing a useful mounting point for armaments.

The fixed wing, whilst it improves manoeuvrability in forward flight, cannot, on its own, significantly increase the maximum forward speed. Additional sources of forward thrust are needed as well.

To increase rotor performance, advanced aerofoil sections are being developed, and more efficient blade shapes are being made possible by the use of fibre-reinforced plastics. These changes simultaneously improve the high lift capability of the blades and allow them to operate closer to the speed of sound. A typical new tip shape, as used in the proposed Westland Lynx 3, is shown in Fig. 9.4.

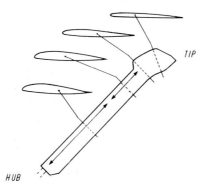

FIG. 9.4 Lynx III main rotor blade showing new tip shape

These changes can significantly improve the performance of existing machines, but do not offer dramatic overall performance gains. One configuration which does is the Advancing Blade Concept (ABC) from Sikorsky. In this case, there are separate hingeless rotors, rotating in opposite directions, on the same shaft. Roll balance is achieved here by developing lift only on the advancing side of each disc. Since these are the blades which speed up as the helicopter accelerates, the available lift increases markedly with speed. It is also now feasible to slow the rotor below the optimum tip speed of Fig. 9.2 because lift is not required from the retreating blades. The absence of a flapping hinge, thereby inhibiting downward blade flapping, makes this acceptable. The effect of this is to increase the maximum obtainable forward speed as well. The performance of this configuration compared with a conventional helicopter is indicated in Fig. 9.5.

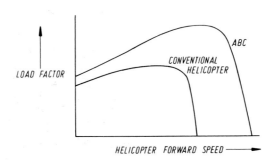

FIG. 9.5 Comparison of load factor on ABC and conventional helicopters

Another advantage of this layout is that, because of the possibility of controlling the yawing of the aircraft by putting different amounts of power into the two rotors, there is no need for a separate tail rotor. There is, therefore, both a power saving and a potential reduction in vehicle length. The latter is illustrated in Fig. 9.6. The removal of the dangerous, and vulnerable, tail rotor is a significant advantage in its own right.

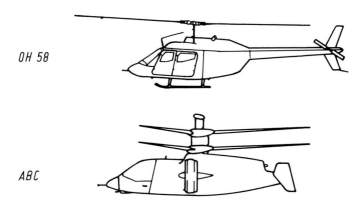

FIG. 9.6 Reduction in length of ABC

The ABC rotor, whilst it offers the possibility of increased forward speed because of the ability to use lower tip speeds, still has a substantially lower forward speed capability than a fixed-wing aircraft, because of the speed additive effects on the advancing blade.

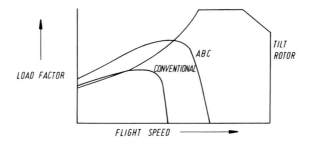

FIG. 9.7 Comparison of load factor on tilt rotor, ABC and conventional helicopters

This disadvantage can be circumvented by using a tilt rotor. This utilises a rotor in the horizontal plane for take-off and landing, just like a helicopter, but for high-speed forward flight the plane of the rotor is tilted forward to become, in effect, a large propeller. This configuration offers aircraft manoeuvrability and forward flight speeds up to say 350 knots, together with a significant improvement in cruise efficiency. Figure 9.7 indicates the kind of performance that can be expected from this type of vehicle.

Flight tests on a representative tilt rotor aircraft, the XV-15, shown in Fig. 9.8 have indicated that the transition from rotor-borne to wing-borne flight can be easily achieved over a wide speed range. The constraints of transition are not, therefore, likely to impose serious operational limitations.

There are other possible aerodynamic developments which offer even greater increases in forward speed coupled with efficient vertical take-off and landing; for example, the X-wing and the Thrust Augmented Wing; but aircraft incorporating these devices are unlikely to be used in the role of a battlefield helicopter and so they will not be discussed further here.

Even without any step changes in aerodynamic design, there will be evolutionary developments aimed at reducing power requirements by, for example, reducing fuselage drag, perhaps by using retractable landing gear, and at increasing control power and reducing maintenance effort with the use of hingeless rotors. With the reductions in airframe and power plant weight described below, the effectiveness of the helicopter on the battlefield will continue to grow.

Engine and Airframe Developments

In round terms, the total weight of a helicopter is made up of three roughly equal parts. These are the weight of the structure and role equipment, the weight of the engine together with some fuel and the weight available for payload. Aerodynamic improvements can offer increases in rotor lift and in aircraft controllability. It is worth pointing out that a 1 per cent increase in rotor thrust will provide a payload increase of about 3 per cent, because of the rough proportionality described above. Another source of improved operational performance would be to reduce either the engine weight or fuel consumption for a given power, or to reduce the structure weight for a given structural strength.

Due, in the main, to increases in engine operating temperature and improvements in component efficiencies, the weight per unit power and the fuel consumption per unit power have both reduced over recent years. The trend of these quantities is shown in Fig. 9.9. It may be expected that this downward trend will continue in the immediate future.

FIG. 9.8 XV-15 tilt rotor aircraft

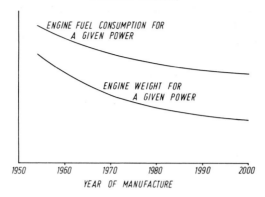

FIG. 9.9 Trends of fuel consumption and weight for given engine power

In the case of the helicopter structure, some significant improvements can be expected in terms of strength and weight, with the use of larger proportions of non-metallic materials and composite materials. Such materials offer several potential advantages over metals. Some materials are directly competitive with structural metals in terms of strength, but these tend to be expensive and difficult to manufacture. At the present time, non-metallic materials are sometimes used for lightly loaded panels, where absolute strength is less important than resistance to buckling. Resistance to buckling is mainly provided by thickness, and this is a good application for honeycomb sandwich materials, which are exceedingly stiff and yet very light.

Another common area for non-metallic materials is for radomes, since glass fibre and other similar composites can be made almost transparent to radio waves. This suggests that another potential advantage of these materials is that their use would reduce the radar signature of the helicopter and by making it more difficult to detect enhance its survivability.

The use of fibre composites introduces the possibility, by laying up the fibres in particular directions, of tailoring the strength of a structural element to the loading it will have to withstand. A very important application in the helicopter is to the rotor blades, the main loading on which is radially outwards.

Of even greater importance for a battlefield vehicle, however, is that some non-metallic elements can be made resistant to impact and blast damage, i.e. the helicopter can be made battle-damage tolerant. With the addition of the corrosion resistance of these materials, the resulting properties make the increased use of non-metallic materials inevitable. Figure 9.10 demonstrates the present trend.

Vibration

The non-uniformity of the velocity distribution along the rotor blades in forward flight necessarily produces periodically fluctuating air loads on the blades as they rotate. The forces and movements which result from this are at particular frequencies, which are dependent upon the rotational speed of the rotor and the number of blades which it contains. Some of these forces are transmitted to the helicopter fuselage and become potent sources of vibration. They may affect parts of the airframe, the flight instruments, the pilot and particularly any sighting and surveillance devices which the helicopter may be carrying. Indeed, it is often the onset of high vibration levels which limits the useful forward speed of present-day helicopters. The trend towards elastomeric bearings and composite blade materials is helpful here, since the increased damping of such materials helps to reduce the amplitude of these vibrations. In addition to this, much effort is currently being devoted to reducing helicopter vibration levels by means such as special rotor mountings and pendulum-type absorbers. The reduced vibration levels thereby attained will also increase helicopter reliability and reduce the maintenance effort required to keep them flying.

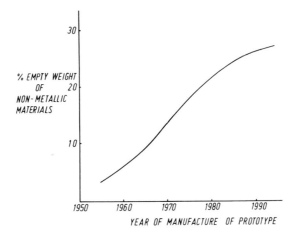

FIG. 9.10 Use of non-metallic materials

Ancillaries

Developments in computerisation and signal processing offer helicopter weapon systems performance enhancement by improving weapon and surveillance and target acquisition capabilities, but these lie outside the scope of this volume.

Future Battlefield Use

Of all battlefield vehicles and weapons systems, the helicopter has enjoyed perhaps the most rapid improvements over the past fifty years. The more advanced types can lift substantial loads or fight alongside ground troops effectively by day and night, in most weather conditions. Imaginative use of these flexible, lethal machines gives commanders an added potential to influence the outcome of any battle. To realise this, however, commanders must be air-minded and be able to recognise the characteristics and shortcomings of the helicopter, no matter how advanced in design these may be.

SELF TEST QUESTIONS

QUESTION 1   What theoretically limits the maximum obtainable forward speed of conventional helicopters?

Answer ....

....

....

....

QUESTION 2   What usually limits the forward speed in practice?

Answer ....

....

....

QUESTION 3   What is the source of helicopter vibration?

Answer ....

....

....

QUESTION 4   What particular problems does vibration in helicopters cause?

Answer ....

....

QUESTION 5   How does manoeuvrability vary with forward speed for a typical helicopter?

Answer ....

....

....

MH—J

QUESTION 6   Why do all helicopters have approximately the same blade tip speed?

Answer ....

....

....

QUESTION 7   How does the ABC rotor achieve increased manoeuvrability and higher forward speeds than a conventional helicopter?

Answer ....

....

....

....

QUESTION 8   Explain the principle of operation of the tilt rotor aircraft.

Answer ....

....

....

....

QUESTION 9   Why does a 1% increase in hovering thrust produce a potential vertical lift payload increase of about 3%?

Answer ....

....

....

....

QUESTION 10 There are at least six potential advantages of using non-metallic
materials in battlefield helicopters. What are they?

Answer ....

....

....

....

....

....

Answers on page 139

Answers to Self Test Questions

Chapter 2

Page 11

QUESTION 1   Since air density decreases with increased altitude, less lift can be generated by the rotor blades. The 'thinner' air also has a detrimental effect on engine performance.

QUESTION 2   In accordance with Bernoulli's theorem, the air passing over the upper surface, having further to travel, speeds up, causing a decrease in pressure. The aerofoil will tend to move towards this lower pressure.

QUESTION 3   Approximately 15°.

QUESTION 4   Drag increases dramatically and the aerofoil stalls.

QUESTION 5   The pilot uses the collective pitch lever to increase the pitch of all the blades, through the swash plate, until the lift produced overcomes the weight of the helicopter. He maintains attitude and direction by using the cyclic stick and rudder pedals, respectively.

QUESTION 6   Drag appears in two basic forms, induced drag and profile drag. Induced drag is created as a result of producing lift: profile drag consist of form (shape) drag and skin friction.

QUESTION 7   The pitch angle of the blades is changed cyclically by the pilot moving the cyclic stick. This action tilts the rotor disc and the total rotor thrust in the same direction as the stick is moved, causing the airframe to move in that direction also.

QUESTION 8   Each blade has three hinges, a flapping hinge, a drag hinge and a feathering hinge.

QUESTION 9   By using a tail rotor or a fenestron. Tail rotors may either push or pull depending on the direction of rotation of the main rotor and which side of the tail fin the tail rotor is mounted. Tail rotors are operated by rudder pedals.

QUESTION 10   A helicopter is in autorotation when there is no power being provided by the engine to the rotors, in flight. The airflow through the rotor disc reverses and the helicopter behaves like an autogyro.

Chapter 3
Page 31
QUESTION 1   a. Observation and reconnaissance.
              b. Armed action.
              c. Direction of fire.
              d. Assistance in command and control.
              e. Movement of men and material.

QUESTION 2   By enabling the helicopter to acquire targets in a 'hull down' or 'turret down' position, they reduce acquisition of the helicopter significantly and thus enhance survivability.

QUESTION 3   Mainly in internal security situations for riot/crowd control. Limited surveillance may also be undertaken.

QUESTION 4   The USA have produced the AH-64 Apache and the USSR have developed the Hind. Italy also has an attack variant under development, the Augusta 129 Mangusta.

QUESTION 5   To carry civilians and large loads over very long distances in their hinterland. They also recognise the military value of large load-carrying helicopters.
QUESTION 6   Airborne early warning, anti-submarine warfare and anti-surface vessel operations.

Chapter 4
Page 49
QUESTION 1   The gas turbine is used almost exclusively.

QUESTION 2   It has an excellent power-to-weight ratio, a very important consideration in helicopters.

QUESTION 3   They are the compressor, combustor and turbine(s), which together provide the net output in the form of a rotating shaft.

QUESTION 4   The two variants are the single-shaft or fixed-turbine engine and the free-turbine type.

QUESTION 5   It is important for both mechanical and aerodynamic reasons that the rotor operates at a substantially constant speed. At too high a speed there is a risk of mechanical failure, while at too low a speed the aerodynamic performance of the rotor deteriorates with a risk of 'coning up' of the blades and a possible catastrophe.

QUESTION 6   The component is an automatic clutch. In the Gazelle, the single-shaft engine must be capable of being disconnected from the rotor during starting. A free-turbine gas generator section can be run up while the turbine and rotor is at rest, since there is no mechanical connection.

QUESTION 7   Because at normal power outputs, which are fairly low, the free-turbine engine can have a reasonably good fuel consumption, while it has the ability to provide a high contingency power in an emergency.

QUESTION 8   By constructing a modular engine it is relatively straightforward to replace a defective module and rapidly return the engine to service, rather than withdraw the complete unit for repair.

QUESTION 9   The pilot looks for good handling characteristics, i.e. the ability to meet his requirements in a safe, rapid and predictable manner.

QUESTION 10   By carefully shielding the exhaust pipe and designing the installation to mix rapidly the exhaust gases with the surrounding air.

Chapter 5
Page 63
QUESTION 1   It is a general term used to describe all the electrical and electronic equipment in a helicopter or aircraft.

QUESTION 2   a.   Artificial Horizon (AH).
               b.   Direction Indicator (DI).
               c.   Turn and Slip Indicator.

QUESTION 3   Angle of descent (glideslope), alignment with the runway (localiser) and distance from touchdown.

QUESTION 4   Two. Doppler systems and inertial navigation systems. Doppler is currently preferred for battlefield helicopters.

QUESTION 5   It relieves the pilot of the immediate task of controlling the helicopter. It is a damping device in pitch and roll and also damps out turbulence by using rate gyroscopes and series actuators.

QUESTION 6   It uses heading, height and airspeed inputs to actually fly the helicopter and can perform all the normal flying functions.

QUESTION 7   Data bus is a system of connecting various sensors by a single pair of wires through a microprocessor, then displaying the information on a VDU.

QUESTION 8   DVI consists of a computer which recognises certain voice patterns, then displays the appropriate information on a video screen. It does away with the need for pushing buttons to select information.

QUESTION 9   A single control handle which performs all the functions of the three sets of conventional controls. It operates by sensing pressure, and does not actually move.

Chapter 6
Page 79
QUESTION 1   They are short-range weapons which would put the helicopter using them at risk. They are also inaccurate when used from helicopters and require much ammunition plus complicated feed/ejection systems.

QUESTION 2   a. Long-range allowing stand-off engagements.
              b. Relatively lightweight.
              c. No recoil problem.
              d. Can be fired from the hover in ambush positions.

QUESTION 3   Integrated Helmet and Display Sight System. It works by sending electrical signals to a slaved turret or weapon, which allows the pilot to sight the weapon instinctively.

QUESTION 4   Through limited finance causing them to select multi-role helicopters rather than the dedicated (but more restricted) attack helicopter.

QUESTION 5   The IR signature is considerably reduced.

QUESTION 6   Laser guided Hellfire missiles, free flight rockets, plus the Hughes 30 mm Chain Gun. A combination of all three can be carried.

QUESTION 7 Forward Looking Infrared.

QUESTION 8 It is not sufficiently armoured to penetrate the FEBA and so is restricted to anti-armour operations behind the FLOT.

QUESTION 9 Their ability to deploy rapidly, unencumbered by terrain, obstacles and conventional routes.

QUESTION 10 Between 10:1 and 19:1, although these rates may be even higher in certain phases of the battle, i.e. counter-penetration.

Chapter 7
Page 95
QUESTION 1 Make it:
a. Difficult to detect.
b. Difficult to hit.
c. Difficult to shoot down.
d. Crashworthy.

QUESTION 2 a. Visual.
b. Acoustic.
c. Radar.
d. Infrared.
e. Electronic.

QUESTION 3 a. Size.
b. Shape.
c. Paint scheme.
d. Transparency glint.
e. Rotor flicker.

QUESTION 4 a. Rapid acceleration and deceleration from and to the hover in all dimensions.
b. The ability to sustain positive G and accept negative G for a few seconds.

QUESTION 5 a. Radar warning receiver.
b. Laser warning receiver.
c. Missile approach detector.
d. Hostile fire indicator.

QUESTION 6 To decoy heat-seeking missiles.

QUESTION 7 By incorporating the following features:
a. Armour plating.
b. Redundancy.

                  c.   Separation.

                  d.   Ballistically tolerant materials.

                  e.   Fire suppression.

QUESTION 8 Because it is heavy and reduces the useful payload which the aircraft could otherwise carry.

QUESTION 9 a. Crashworthy fuel tanks.
                  b. Tanks positioned away from ignition sources.
                  c. Breakaway valves.

QUESTION 10 a. Cost-effectiveness.
                  b. Weight.
                  c. Volume.
                  d. Power requirements.
                  e. Maintenance and logistic requirements.

Chapter 8
Page 109

QUESTION 1 Composite materials have the following advantages:
                  a. Lighter.
                  b. Longer fatigue life.
                  c. Less maintenance.
                  d. Greater ballistic tolerance.
                  e. Easier to shape and manufacture.

QUESTION 2 a. Lower fuel consumption.
                  b. Reduced weight.
                  c. Greater reliability.
                  d. Less maintenance.
                  e. Easier/quicker to start.

QUESTION 3 a. Engines can be run closer to limits.
                  b. Automatic torque matching.
                  c. On-condition monitoring.
                  d. Automatic starting.

QUESTION 4 Fly-by-wire or fly-by-light.

QUESTION 5 a. Warning the pilot.
                  b. Wire cutters built into the airframe.
                  c. Wire deflectors.

QUESTION 6   a.   Less exposure of the helicopter to the enemy.
                 b.   Almost 360° view.
                 c.   Eliminates C of G problems that arise with other locations, i.e. well forward in the roof.

QUESTION 7   a.   TV camera.
                 b.   LLTV camera.
                 c.   LRF/LTM.
                 d.   Thermal imager.

QUESTION 8   3−5 and 8−14 micrometres.

QUESTION 9   Starlight.

Chapter 9
Page 121

QUESTION 1   The theoretical limit to helicopter forward speed comes from a combination of aerofoil stall at the tip of the retreating blade and compressibility drag rise at the tip of the advancing blade. These effects lead to a loss of lift, a substantial increase in power required and rotor vibration.

QUESTION 2   Maximum speed of a helicopter is usually determined by the high levels of vibration experienced as the speed is increased. This speed is often well below the theoretical speed limit referred to above.

QUESTION 3   Helicopter vibration is caused by the difference in air speed on the advancing and retreating blades of the rotor in forward flight. This produces rapidly changing airloads and hence blade vibrations which are transmitted through the rotor hub to the helicopter fuselage.

QUESTION 4   Vibration can cause airframe and pilot fatigue, make instruments inoperable or unreadable and render sighting and surveillance devices ineffective.

QUESTION 5   Above a rather low speed, the manoeuvrability of a helicopter falls very rapidly with forward speed (see Fig. 9.3). This is due to the effects of rotor horizontal translation summarised in the answer to Question 1.

QUESTION 6   All manned helicopters have approximately the same tip speed due to the combination of retreating blade stall and advancing blade Mach number effects considered in the answer to Question 1. This is illustrated in Fig. 9.2.

QUESTION   7   The Advancing Blade Concept achieves roll balance by using
                the lift on the advancing side only of two coaxial rotors
                rotating in opposite directions. This increases the lift available
                since the loss of lift on the retreating side of the disc is no
                longer a limiting factor on the total lift available nor on the
                maximum attainable forward speed.

QUESTION   8   The tilt-rotor aircraft uses its rotors in the horizontal plane
                like a helicopter for low-speed and hovering flight, but tilts
                them to the vertical for high-speed forward flight. This
                removes all of the helicopter speed limitations described above
                since these are caused by movement of the rotor disc in the
                same plane as the blade rotation.

QUESTION   9   In the hover, the thrust of the helicopter rotor must be
                identical to the total weight of the helicopter. Therefore, a 1%
                increase in hovering thrust will allow the all up weight to
                increase by 1%. If everything else remains unchanged, this
                will appear as a relative increase approximately three times
                larger in the payload, which is approximately one third of the
                all up weight.

QUESTION 10   The potential benefits of non-metallic materials are:
                a. They may be made lighter for the same strength, particu-
                    larly in thin-skinned areas.
                b. They may be made almost transparent to radio waves.
                c. Their strength, stiffness and shape may be easily tailored
                    for special applications e.g. rotor blades.
                d. They can be made resistant to impact and blast damage.
                e. They are corrosion resistant.
                f. They possess high inherent damping which helps to reduce
                    the effects of vibration.

Glossary of Terms and Abbreviations

A

ABC
:   Advancing Blade Concept.

ACAP
:   Advanced Composite Airframe Programme.

ACT
:   Active Control Technology.

ADOCS
:   Advanced Digital Optical Control System.

Aerofoil section
:   The cross-sectional shape of a wing designed to produce lift and minimise drag.

AFCS
:   Automatic Flight Control System.

Agility
:   Rapid acceleration and deceleration in all directions.

AH
:   Artificial Horizon (also Attitude Indicator).

Airframe
:   The components which make up the structure of a helicopter.

Armed helicopter
:   A multi-role helicopter which is armed with one or a number of weapons for its own use.

ASI
:   Airspeed Indicator.

MH–K

ASV
>Anti-surface Vessel.

ASW
>Anti-submarine warfare.

ATGW
>Anti-tank Guided weapons.

Attack helicopter
>A helicopter which is specifically designed to operate only in a fighting role.

Autogyro
>A machine which uses the action of a freely rotating rotor to fly. An engine for forward thrust is also used.

Autopilot
>A closed loop system in which accelerometers and gyroscopes control the flight of a helicopter.

Autorotation
>The free rotation of a rotor resulting from an inflow of air upwards through the rotor disc due to the helicopter descending.

Autostabiliser
>A damping device in pitch and roll without the authority to hold a given datum. It also damps out turbulence.

Axial flow compressor
>A compressor in which the flow of air is parallel to the axis of the shaft.

B

Barometric altimeter
>An altimeter which uses barometric pressure as a means of indicating height

BERP
>British Experimental Rotor Project.

Black Hole concept
>A system which rapidly mixes ambient air with jet effluxes to reduce the IR signature of engines.

BMMS

    Battlefield Mission Management System.

    C

Centrifugal compressor

    A compressor which draws air in at its centre and forces this through radial vanes to exit at its periphery.

Chaff

    A large number of dipole reflectors which, when discharged, disguise the radar signature of a helicopter.

Collective pitch

    Uniform and simultaneous application of pitch to all the main rotor blades.

Combuster

    A chamber where a mixture of fuel and air is burned.

Compound helicopter

    A helicopter which has either fixed wings or propulsive engines, or both these, in addition to a conventional rotor.

Compressor

    An aerodynamic rotational device which raises the pressure of air passing through it.

Cyclic pitch

    The physical blade angle which varies as the blade rotates.

    D

Data bus

    A system of connecting various sensors through a microprocessor to present information to the pilot.

Fenestron

    A tail rotor set within a tail fin, similar to a ducted fan.

Fixed turbine

    A turbine which is fixed directly to the output shaft.

Flapping hinge
>A hinge at the root of a rotor blade which allows it to move up and down freely.

FLIR
>Forward Looking Infrared.

Fly-by-wire/fly-by-light
>Flying controls where mechanical linkages are replaced by electronic or light links.

Free turbine
>A turbine which has no mechanical connection to the gas generator.

Fully articulated rotor
>A rotor system in which the main rotor blades have flapping, drag and feathering hinges.

G

Gas generator
>The principle working parts of a gas turbine engine.

Glideslope
>The angle of descent of an aircraft relative to a fixed point on the ground.

H

Hellfire
>A laser-guided anti-tank missile.

DI
>Direction Indicator.

Direct Voice Input (DVI)
>A voice recognition system which displays information when interrogated by a pilot.

Disymmetry of lift
>Unequal lift generated by a helicopter's main rotor blades due to the forward speed of the aircraft.

Drag
> The force which opposes motion.

Drag hinge
> A hinge at the root of the rotor blade which allows restricted movement in azimuth.

E

Elastomeric bearings
> Bearings which consist of alternate layers of metal shims and a rubber compound called elastomer.

F

FADEC
> Full Authority Digital Engine Control.

Feathering hinge
> A hinge at the root of the rotor blade about which changes in pitch angle are made.

Higher Hormonic Control (HHC)
> A computer controlled vibration suppression system.

I

IHADSS
> Integrated Helmet and Display Sight System.

IR
> Infrared electromagnetic radiation.

ILS
> Instrument Landing System.

Induced drag
> Drag created by forward movement of a body: it is the penalty for having lift.

ISA

International Standard Atmosphere.

L

Laser

Light Amplification by Stimulated Emission of Radiation.

Lift

Force at right angles to the direction of motion: it overcomes weight and provides a manoeuvre capability.

Load factor

Ratio of lift to weight.

Localiser

The alignment of an aircraft in azimuth to a fixed datum on the ground (normally the centre line of a runway).

M

Mast mounted sight

A sight which is mounted directly above the main rotor hub.

P

Parasite drag

The retarding force on a moving body caused by the shape of the body plus skin friction.

Precession

The angular change of the plane of rotation of a gyroscope under the action of an applied force.

Pressure (pitot) head

A device which feeds static and dynamic pressure to certain flight instruments.

R

Rate gyroscope

A two frame gyroscope with freedom about its spinning axis and about an axis perpendicular to the spinning axis, which is restrained by springs.

Rigid rotor
>   A main rotor system in which the blades do not have hinges (also bearingless rotor).

RWR
>   Radar Warning Receiver.

S

SACLOS
>   Semi-automatic Command to Line of Sight.

SAR
>   Search and Rescue.

Semi-rigid rotor
>   A main rotor system in which the blades have only one hinge.

Sidearm control
>   A single force feel control which performs all the functions of conventional helicopter controls.

Skin friction
>   Friction which is set up when relative motion exists between a body and air.

Specific fuel consumption (sfc)
>   An air-breathing engine performance parameter defined as fuel flow rate divided by net thrust.

Stall
>   The phenomenon which causes an aircraft to lose height because of a loss of lift and an increase in drag.

Swept tip
>   The angling rearwards of the tip section of a rotor blade or wing.

T

TADS/PNVS
>   Target Acquisition and Designation Sight/Pilots Night Vision Sensor.

Tail rotor
>   An anti-torque device.

TANS

Tactical Air Navigation System.

TAS

True Airspeed.

Thermodynamic efficiency

The ratio of energy output of an engine to the energy content of the fuel.

Tilt wing

A design which rotates the rotor and wing to which it is attached through a 90° upward arc.

Torque

The equal and opposite reaction of the fuselage around the axis of the main rotor shaft, to the rotational movement of the main rotor.

Total rotor thrust

The force produced by the main rotor at 90° to its plane of rotation.

TOW

Tube launched, optically tracked, wire guided. A semi-automatic anti-tank missile.

Turbine

A device which extracts energy from a flow of gas to provide a power output.

Turboshaft

A gas turbine engine which produces power through a rotating output shaft.

V

VSI

Vertical Speed Indicator.

W

Watt

A unit of power (joules/second).

X

X Wing

A development project in which the main rotor is locked in forward flight to produce lift like a fixed wing aircraft.

Bibliography

MUNSON, K., *Helicopters and other Rotorcraft Since 1907,* Blandford Colour Series, London.

GUNSTON, W., *Aviation, The Story of Flight,* St Michael.

FAY, J., *The Helicopter History, Piloting and How It Flies,* David and Charles.

The Aerodynamics of Low Speed Aircraft and Helicopters, RMCS.

Index